I0184427

Praise for **BALD**

"Kate Bigwood Atkinson takes us behind the scenes of her medical story with clarity, humor and faith. BALD underscores the plain facts that science and medicine are galloping forward and attitude matters. Kate Atkinson's words underscore the idea that we each do better in good times and bad when we nurture an interdependent web of family, friends and supporters. To be deeply alive is to face our happy times and our challenges with equal measure of presence and grace, compellingly illustrated in this book. A terrific read."

Dr. Amy Rothenberg
Author of *You Finished Treatment, Now What?
A Field Guide for Cancer Survivors*

"With BALD Kate Bigwood Atkinson demonstrates the importance of faith and hope and human connection as antidotes to fear and uncertainty following multiple cancer diagnoses and rigorous medical interventions. Her reliance on unflagging humor and a wealth of sustaining memories and experiences results in a revealing, amusing, and inspiring memoir of a challenging period within a life devoted to serving church and community."

Margaret Porter, Bestselling Author

"Kate Bigwood Atkinson sees how illness and uncertain outcome have widened her window into the experience of those she finds around her. She shows how a meaningful way through her own trials is by deeply engaging with fellow travelers."

Frederick M. Briccetti, M.D., Oncologist

BALD

Confronting Cancer and Living Large

Kate Bigwood Atkinson

Copyright © Kate Bigwood Atkinson 2024
All rights reserved
ISBN: 979-8-9907172-0-6

For Michael

Chapter One
What Happened?

My mother often declared, "We don't do cancer. We're a cardio-pulmonary family."

Then she was diagnosed with multiple myeloma.

Once she got over the surprise of her diagnosis—surprise, not shock, because my mother took most things in her stride, including cancer—she became determined to make the most of whatever life she had left. To quote Frank Sinatra, my mother planned to "live until she died."

And that's what she did for four years. She served on committees, she sang in a choir, she visited her children, she had her hair and nails done, she went to the movies, she played bridge, and she auditioned for "Who Wants to be a Millionaire." (She passed the written test but didn't make the cut.)

The day before she died, my mother attended a leaving party for the rector of her church, and only began to feel unwell when she returned home. She was in hospice care by then: a favorite of the nurses because she was so much fun. That evening, when severe pain set in, they gave her morphine and did everything they could to keep her comfortable. She was in a coma for a day then quietly slipped away.

She lived until she died.

Eight years later, I had surgery for squamous cell tumors. My right tonsil was removed, along with a lymph node. Four years after that, I was diagnosed with mantle cell lymphoma.

Apparently, our family does do cancer.

Chapter Two
Change of Plans

I am an Episcopal priest, ordained in 1996, and for over 13 years, serving as rector of St. Catherine's, a large, city center parish in New England, affectionately known as St. Cat's.

One of the benefits of being full-time clergy in the Episcopal Church is a three-month sabbatical every five to seven years. It had been six years since my last sabbatical, and, because there was a lot going on in the parish, I decided to take my leave in two halves: six weeks in the spring, and six weeks in the fall.

Part two of my sabbatical was scheduled to begin in the middle of September, and, though I'd not yet planned much for those six weeks away from the parish, I had made the necessary arrangements for clergy coverage during that time. And that was a good thing—because, by the time the official start date rolled around, I knew I had cancer.

In this Corona age, even being fully vaccinated and boosted was no guarantee of immunity to that sneaky virus. I had only recently succumbed to it—having started to believe I'd avoided it, until those two little lines appeared on my home test. I was, unknowingly, in stage four cancer by then, but I blamed my exhaustion on COVID-19. I'd also been bothered by a swelling in my neck, which had appeared around nine months previously. But I hadn't worried too much about it because a needle aspiration biopsy that spring had indicated "no evidence of malignancy."

But the lump wasn't going anywhere. In fact, it was getting bigger. Then another lump appeared, on the other side of my neck. A camera down the back of my throat revealed a malignant tumor, and I was scheduled for a surgical biopsy to find out what kind of cancer I had.

It became clear that what was originally planned to be six weeks of refreshment, study, and otherwise uplifting activities, would in fact be medical leave.

Even before the biopsy took place, my doctors told me the bald truth. There would be chemotherapy, along with which there would be side effects: weakness, fatigue, nausea, hair-thinning, and an increased susceptibility to whatever germs might be floating around. I'm no athlete, but I am generally strong and healthy—and I was about to become weak and sick.

The biopsy was horrible. Going in through my mouth, the surgeon removed a sizable chunk of the tumor lodged behind my remaining tonsil. When I came out of the anesthesia, the pain was indescribable, like a cluster of razor blades in my throat, and, for several weeks after the surgery, I could only manage to swallow liquids. But the doctors got what they needed. I had my diagnosis, and I would soon have a treatment plan.

Until that time, I had been under the impression that there were only two types of lymphoma: Hodgkin's and non-Hodgkin's. It turns out there are multiple versions of non-Hodgkin's, and, when the results of the biopsy came back, I discovered that I had myself a doozy: the rare and aggressive mantle cell lymphoma.

The good thing about doozies is that doctors and research scientists don't like them, so they put a lot of time and effort into finding cures for them. Twenty, even ten years ago mantle cell lymphoma. would probably have meant a death sentence for me, but, thanks to a substantial investment of those experts' time and effort, I would be undergoing a treatment that was extensively tested and refined: six months of chemotherapy, followed by a stem cell transplant, followed by three years of maintenance chemo. Two oncologists would be caring for me, the primary one at Dana Farber in Boston, and the other in my hometown.

"When your time comes, Kate, you will die of old age," both doctors assured me independently. "We fully intend to cure you."

That was the level of confidence that sustained me as I started my journey, but there were moments when I was not at all sure that I would be cured, moments of doubt, and fear, and anger, and frustration. And, running through it all, I was experiencing a deep, agonizing sense of loss.

Chapter Three
A Chapter Closes

As the six weeks of clergy coverage drew to a close at St. Cat's, and my chemotherapy treatments began to take their toll, my Bishop informed me that he had lined up a retired priest to take over the day-to-day running of the parish. He also recommended that I retire when my short-term disability benefit had finished—in less than five months.

I was devastated.

And yet, I knew he was right. At age 66, I was already past an acceptable retirement age—and, in fact, I had a tentative plan in place to retire when I reached age 68. But retirement from a parish one has served for more than 13 years usually means making an announcement at least three months ahead of time, then spending those three months tying up loose ends, completing projects, preparing a hand-over, and, most important of all, saying goodbye to beloved parishioners.

Leave-taking is a process. Cancer robbed me of that.

St. Cat's is alive with ministries to people living with mental health challenges, bereavement, illness, poverty, homelessness, addiction, and hopelessness. It's a parish that celebrates its faith in numerous, wonderful ways—including music, fellowship, education, spiritual growth, diversity, generous giving, service, laughter, and pastoral care.

If I had to define my primary role as a priest, it would be "Minister of Encouragement."

Whenever I looked out at my congregation, from the pulpit or the altar, something amazing happened: I would experience a wave of overwhelming love that encompassed every person in sight. I knew many of my congregants well, of course, but there were always some who were fairly new to the parish, or even there for the first time that day. As well as that, there would invariably be a handful of parishioners who had annoyed me somehow, at some time. It didn't matter. I loved them all, equally and unreservedly.

That kind of love isn't self-generated; it couldn't possibly be. As flawed human beings, try as we may, our love for one another tends to come with rules and conditions. Genuinely unconditional love is God-given.

I'm not the only one, of course, but God has blessed me with the capacity to love others the way God loves us—unconditionally. That gift has made all the difference in my parish ministry.

A ministry of encouragement means expressing God's love in every personal encounter; it also means building people up, boosting their dignity, and helping them to see their worth as unique individuals, beloved children of God. And it means helping others to recognize their own gifts for ministry, and to put them to good use. One of my favorite—and probably over-used—observations is that you don't need a piece of plastic around your neck to be a minister.

A truly healthy congregation is aware that the church is not the building, it's the people. And, as those people discover just how well-equipped they are to do God's work, the church becomes stronger and stronger; and its ministries become less and less constrained by the walls of the building. My greatest joy, over more than a decade serving at St. Cat's, was seeing individuals progress from Sunday worshipper, to ministry team member, to fully involved lay minister—often ending up in a leadership role. My main responsibility as rector had been to assist in that process.

And, all of a sudden, it was taken away from me.

But I am my mother's daughter, and I was not going to let mantle cell lymphoma get the better of me. A month before my short-term disability benefit came to an end, I announced my retirement to the parish.

> *Dear parish family,*
>
> *As most of you know, I had an unexpected cancer diagnosis last summer and have been receiving treatment since mid-September. I will have my final round of chemotherapy in just under a month, then, at the end of April, I'll be admitted to Dana Farber Hospital for a stem cell transplant. Because my immune system will be non-functioning for many months following the transplant, it will be necessary for me to remain isolated at Dana Farber for two to three weeks and then at home for the duration.*
>
> *Because of this situation, I have made the difficult decision to retire as rector of St. Cat's, effective March 14th.*
>
> *Before my diagnosis I had made tentative retirement plans for two years from now, which would have given us all time to prepare for my*

leaving and to say our goodbyes. For me, the hardest part of my pending departure is the absence of that time of preparation.

I hope you will continue to be present— participating in worship services, taking full advantage of the wide variety of formation offerings, getting involved in new areas of lay ministry, and spending time together, getting to know one another better and celebrating the joy of this remarkable community that is St. Cat's Episcopal Church.

Thank you for all the joy you have given me over the years. I carry you in my heart, now and always.

God bless you, and love from Kate.

I had been on medical leave for more than five months by the time I wrote my letter, so, in the eyes of many, perhaps, I was already gone. However, I had missed out on one of the most important elements of parish ministry—and so had my peeps.

The absence of a proper farewell was only part of my feeling of loss. How would I fill the empty days that stretched ahead of me, with nothing to look forward to other than aggressive treatments, long weeks away from my home and loved ones, and enforced isolation for months on end while my body fought to regain its strength and immunity?

Worst of all was the loss of my vocation, the ministry that had fed me, and had enriched the lives of so many. I simply was not ready to give up that huge part of who I am—and yet, it appeared as though that was exactly what I had to do.

But I was wrong. As it happens, you can take the priest out of the church, but you can't take the church out of the priest!

Chapter Four
Customer Relations

My transplant journey began the morning of the last day of April. Michael folded his tall frame into our Subaru, and the three of us, Michael and I, and our Cavalier King Charles Spaniel, Ernie, drove to Boston.

Despite leaving early, we failed to avoid Sunday traffic—because everyone else was already driving home from weekend getaways spoiled by rain. Michael's grim expression reflected the driving conditions.

He had been brave and strong throughout my ordeal, but the stress was visible in the tightness of his mouth, and a haunted look in his eyes. The time had come for us to undergo the most critical part of my treatment. If it weren't successful, I might have a death sentence after all. Michael's jaw was clenched beneath the beard he grew during the pandemic. My handsome husband carried a heavy burden of worry.

Although he'd been careful not to voice his fears, in order to protect me, I know he was thinking about the possibility of losing his life partner, and having to face the remainder of his life alone. How I longed to take away those dark musings—but the truth was, I was scared too. Even knowing that we were heading for a center of extraordinary medical excellence, the possibility of failure was never far from our thoughts.

I was newly bald. I had followed the recommendation of my "Nurse Navigator" to have my head shaved in advance of losing my hair. As a long-standing member of my oncology team, her experience had taught her that it's much tidier to forestall the inevitable hair loss by taking care of it oneself. She was right. It also meant that I could send my shoulder-blade-length locks to an organization that makes wigs for cancer patients.

For other cancer patients, that is. I had looked into the possibility of having my hair made into a wig for myself, but I discovered a) that it would cost me $400 - $500, and b) that it takes at least three heads of hair to make a single wig, and I only have one.

By the time we reached our destination, I was both bald and worn out from the car journey. You would have thought these would be dead give-aways, when checking into a Boston hotel, that we were not there to party. Many of those hotels even offer "medical rates" for guests like me who are in town for treatment at one of the city's world-renowned hospitals.

While Michael busied himself getting our luggage out of the car and wrangling Ernie, who often needs to pee at inconvenient times, I attempted to check us in.

"I'm very sorry, Ma'am," said the young man at the reception desk—not sounding in the least bit sorry— "but I'm afraid I have no record of a reservation in your name."

"We made our reservation online, and pre-paid…" I began, but he interrupted.

"As I said, we have no reservation for you. I have checked twice. We have rooms available, of course, but we can't put you in one without a reservation. I'm very sorry. Now, if you'll excuse me."

He turned away, and began examining some papers.

I had reached the point where I could no longer stand up straight, and was leaning heavily on the counter in an effort to avoid collapsing in a heap. I was obviously a sick and exhausted woman.

After a long moment, he looked up again and sighed when he saw me still standing there. "You could call the company you booked with, Ma'am, and perhaps find proof of your reservation?"

Right. On a Sunday afternoon.

But I did as I was told and made the call.

Sure enough, I got a recording saying the office was closed. But, wonder of wonders, there was an option to leave a message if you were "having a problem with check-in."

I confess that I wasn't very hopeful, but I did my best.

Barely managing to hold back tears, I identified myself and the name of the hotel.

"I'm in Boston for cancer treatment and I'm trying to check in, but the desk clerk says he has no record of our reservation. He says he can't give us a room without proof that we've already booked and paid for one."

"Please," I continued, feeling sick and beginning to choke up, "I really need to get into my room and lie down. Could someone please... call ...me back? Please?"

Voice shaking, I completed the call and collapsed on a bench. My tears were flowing by this time, attracting some odd looks from passing patrons—who presumably had been permitted to check into *their* rooms. After a few minutes, Michael and Ernie found me there, and did their best to comfort me—Michael by enfolding me in his arms, and Ernie by leaping into my lap and licking my nose.

Then, wonder of wonders, I got a call back from an agent, with a very soothing voice. "Mrs. Atkinson," she began, "I've been in touch with the manager of your hotel. I provided him with proof of your reservation, and, to compensate for your inconvenience, he has waived all your extra fees— including the daily pet charge."

I fell in love with the agent on the spot. "I can't thank you enough," I said, and thanked her again, profusely.

Nearly an hour after our arrival, we finally got into our room, ordered dinner from an Indian restaurant, and settled down for the night.

Full to bursting with chicken tikka masala, saag paneer, and dog food, Michael and I, and Ernie, went to sleep.

The next day, a new chapter of this journey would begin—and it would be very different from the last time.

Chapter Five: T-Day Minus Ten
Round One

"Last time" was close to five years previously, when I had noticed a lump in the right side of my neck. It felt a little like a marble, rolling around under my fingers, like the swollen glands I used to get as a kid whenever I caught a cold. I didn't worry about it, but I did show it to my doctor the next time I saw her, and she wasn't concerned either.

But my neck marble didn't go away; instead, it appeared to be growing. It was beginning to bother me enough that I committed the unmannerly act of asking a member of my parish, who happened to be a doctor, if she would feel the growth and tell me what she thought. She, too, was unconcerned, as well as very gracious about my faux pas.

"Okay," I remember thinking, "I have a lump in my neck but it's nothing to worry about."

That bit of reassurance didn't stop me from bringing it up again at my annual physical. This time my doctor's response was different. She kept her fingers on my neck for nearly a minute, moving them around, palpating, and all the while muttering a string of possible causes for what was now a golf ball-sized lump.

Finally, she said, "I'm sending you to Dr. Hammer, an ear, nose, and throat specialist."

Amazingly, I found myself in his chair less than two weeks later!

Things slowed down after that. I had three or four appointments with Dr. Hammer over the summer, during which time he didn't appear to do much more than palpate my lump and order an ultrasound. One consultation was so completely lacking in progress that I asked for a refund of my co-pay. (I got it.) It wasn't until mid- September, that Dr. Hammer performed a needle biopsy on my, by then, plum-sized lump.

Throughout this time, I was positive that whatever was going on in my neck, it was not cancer. It was an overactive gland, or a cyst, or a benign tumor, but it was not cancer.

I was wrong.

My birthday is at the end of September, and Michael, our teenaged daughter, Alex, and I, had planned a special weekend trip to Manhattan. We had tickets for *Pretty Woman*, the stage musical version of one of our favorite movies. We were going to travel to the city on the Friday bus, check into our hotel, grab some dinner, and go to the show.

On Thursday evening, I received a phone call. The one I'd been waiting for: "Mrs. Atkinson, it's Dr. Hammer."

I sat down.

"Uh, we have received your biopsy results. Yes. Mrs. Atkinson... they show that things have... metastasized, that is, there are malignant cells... in your lymph node."

"What does that mean?" I asked, knowing what it meant.

"I'm sorry, but we can't tell you any more until you have a PET scan. We'll set that up right away."

I had cancer. And it had metastasized.

I told Michael right away. I felt cold all over, and trembling even though I wasn't visibly shaking. I'll never forget the look on my sweet husband's face, as it drained of color and his eyes filled with tears. For a few minutes, neither of us made any sense because we were both trying to talk without saying what was really on our minds.

"I'll put gas in the car… for you," Michael offered.

"Oh, that's okay… I mean, do you think it needs it? I mean to go for the… PET scan?"

I was terrified that I was going to abandon my husband and teenage daughter; Michael was terrified that he was going to lose his wife. Those fears remained unspoken, but we both wept in each other's arms.

What we did not do was tell Alex what was going on. She would find out soon enough, and we didn't want to spoil the special occasion that we'd been looking forward to for so long.

Instead, I called my sister.

Four years younger than I am, Joanie has lived through countless health crises with her big sister. For some reason, I am the one of four siblings who gets everything. It started, as a teen, with back surgeries—one of which required four months in bed, while the second called for six months on my back in a body cast. At age 21, I had my gall bladder removed; later came more back surgery, fistula repair, hysterectomy, benign ovarian tumor removal, internal hernia repair, and numerous less invasive maladies.

My little sister is herself bursting with health, and she has plenty of energy and strength to spare, every time I find myself facing a new hurdle. She also researches my symptoms on the internet, something I deliberately avoid.

So I called her, and there was more weeping. Just the word "cancer" is scary. When you start to imagine all the possible outcomes, it's terrifying. But the thing about Joanie and me is that we laugh. We laugh a lot. It's not like we deny whatever unpleasant things may be going on in our lives, but we are able to appreciate humor at the same time. And that is a wonderful thing when terror is lurking.

On this distressful occasion, Joanie still had a funny story about our mother—who we affectionately called Muth (pronounced like mother but without the "er").

"Remember when I told Muth to be sure to share her 'dying wishes' with her loved ones?" Joanie said. "And a little later, she did? She said, 'Honey, I have a dying wish.' And I asked her, all serious, 'What is it?'"

The pair of us cracked up, in unison, as we recited Muth's dying wish: "Can you get me a Kleenex?"

But there was more. Joanie reminded me of the time when she brought her two children to visit Muth (known to the children as Grandy), and the topic arose again. "What's your dying wish for me, Grandy?" asked my niece.

"Don't play with your hair," Grandy replied.

"How come I don't get a dying wish?" asked my nephew.

"It's the same as your sister's," was her short reply.

We laughed hard over our mother's antics; once again, Joanie's stories had lifted my spirits, at least for the time being.

......

In the early days of that first cancer, I found it especially difficult to pray—which surprised me. I was going through one of the greatest challenges of my life so far. And I was scared.

But it is precisely at times like those that we need God the most. After all, we have God's promises to rely on, found in some of the most familiar verses of scripture:

> *"Though I walk through the valley of the shadow of death, I will fear no evil, for you are with me..."* Psalm 23:4

> And *"I am with you always, until the end of days."* Matthew 28:20

I have pointed to those words countless times when offering comfort to parishioners in distress. And yet I found myself unable to turn to my loving, faithful God. Why?

Possibly I just didn't know what to say. I knew beyond doubt that God did not give me cancer. In this life, illness, injury, sorrow, fear, and all kinds of evil and pain exist. They are simply a part of living in an imperfect world. It's the next life which contains none of those things. It breaks my heart when people who are hurting ask, "Why is God doing this to me?" because God never causes   suffering.

I knew God would give me the strength to get through my ordeal—because that's what God does—but I couldn't find the words to say so in prayer.

I needn't have worried. Many of my nearest and dearest were praying on my behalf. And God doesn't always have to hear us put our needs into words—especially when we've been temporarily struck dumb—because God already knows and understands what those needs are.

Thank God!

Now, four and a half years later, I was ready to get into the ring again and do my part in defeating my latest cancer opponent. Mantle cell lymphoma, look out.

And then it was Monday, and the count-down began in earnest.

Chapter Six: T-Day Minus Nine
Conscious Sedation

Stem cell transplant patients live by a calendar that's all our own. It begins with a countdown to the day of transplant (Day Zero, or T-Day) and continues with a count-up to the critical thirtieth day post-transplant (T-Day+30). My countdown began on Sunday, with our nearly abortive arrival at our hotel, and continued the next morning, with appointments on various floors of Boston's Dana Farber Cancer Institute (DFCI), and Brigham and Women's Hospital (BWH).

The main attraction for this day, other than blood draws and a COVID test (negative), was the installation of my central line. Not to be confused with my port—which still resides, quite prominently (although subcutaneously) in the upper right corner of my chest—the central line was threaded into a vein under my left shoulder bone. The tube leading from the vein was visible under my skin, and it emerged in the form of a patriotic (red, white, and blue) trio of IV hubs that I will for evermore refer to as "dingle-dangles."

The placement of the line is done by a radiologist, who follows its progress using x-ray technology. The patient is given the kind of sedative we over-50s know and love from colonoscopies—the one where you allegedly stay awake and watch the camera's progression through your lower gut. But I have never heard of anyone managing to stay awake and watch their colonoscopy. So why is it called conscious sedation?

Just in case I did have the audacity to stay awake and watch my central line placement, my head was draped in a sort of tent which prevented me from seeing anything other than the midsection of one of the attending technicians. I was consciously sedated for long enough to feel some rummaging around beneath my collarbone—no pain though—then off I went to la-la land.

I was scheduled for one final procedure on T-Day minus nine. My bloodwork had indicated a rather measly showing of stem cells in my bloodstream, so it was necessary to give me an injection of plerixafor. I learned that this is a stimulant that would encourage more of my stem cells to leave the comfort of my bone marrow and start swimming around freely—with no inkling of what was in store for them over the next few days.

Once my central line was in place, the effects of the sedative wore off and I was fully conscious and alert. With more than an hour's wait for my plerixafor shot, I decided to go for a walk. There's not much to see in that part of Boston, unless one is a devotee of tall medical buildings. It was, however, a chance for me to be alone with my thoughts in the middle of what felt like a whirlwind of events beyond my control.

I had experienced another whirlwind of events four years earlier, when we set off for the Big Apple to celebrate my 62nd birthday. It was one of those occasions life is full of, when wonderful things happen at exactly the same time as awful things. I had an as yet unidentified cancer growing in my body; still, Friday's dinner was delicious, Pretty Woman was very true to the film—with that great scene of Rodeo Drive shopping, plus original songs—and

Michael and I were able to banish our dark thoughts for at least some of the time.

Alex, in blissful ignorance, had a blast spending our money in various tourist traps. She selected numerous little New York license plates bearing the names of all her friends—including several I didn't even recognize. She found a purse made from a dozen zippers interspersed with narrow ribbons of fabric (a style I found confusing because I would never know which zipper to open), and an "I heart NY" sweatshirt. Also, fake tattoos, a Big Apple snow globe, and a selection of branded pencils. I was unusually free and easy with my credit card. Perhaps I thought that inundating our daughter with gifts would make up for what she would find out before long.

Or maybe I just needed the distraction. I do know that I took a lot of showers that weekend. The shower is a good place to cry.

Our bus back home left early afternoon the next day, which was my actual birthday, and we had arranged to meet a college friend, Ashley, for brunch beforehand. Knowing we didn't have to drive, Michael, Ashley, and I ordered cocktails as a celebratory treat. We had taken maybe two sips of our respective drinks when the server arrived with a chilled bottle of champagne! During our phone conversation the other day, Joanie had cunningly extracted from me the name of the brunch restaurant. Then she and my two brothers had arranged our bottle of bubbly as a birthday surprise.

I knew it was also my siblings' way of saying, "We're so sorry you have cancer."

Their thoughtful gesture nearly brought me to tears—without the benefit of a shower in which to hide them.

Happily, there was a great deal of humor to be found in the challenge for each of us to consume both a generous cocktail, and a third of a bottle of champagne. We giggled our way through brunch, much to Alex's embarrassment, then Michael and I poured ourselves onto the bus home. Alex sat as far away from us as she possibly could.

At the hospital the following Monday, I had a full body PET scan but the results left Dr. Hammer no better informed. The only cancer that showed up was the secondary growth in my lymph node—and we already knew about that. There was no sign of a primary site.

The next step in identifying and treating that first cancer, was a referral to the Head and Neck clinic at Mass Eye and Ear Infirmary (MEE), in Boston. Once again, I got an appointment almost immediately, and was soon being examined by a dashing young doctor. He put a camera down my nose, and his fingers down my throat, and instantly diagnosed a squamous cell cancer in my right tonsil. (This is one of the cancers that can be caused by the human papilloma virus, which has made me a determined advocate for the HPV vaccine.)

Little did I know, when I was referred to MEE, that my doctor there had been recruited because of his expertise in surgical treatment of my particular cancer. Using a specialized robot that looked a lot like an octopus, he would excise the cancerous cells, including my tonsil and lymph node, after which I would almost certainly have no need of chemo nor radiotherapy. I didn't.

Due to the demand for operating theatres, my surgeon was, at that time, only performing this surgery one day a month—but I had a request.

In addition to the trip to New York, my main birthday gift had been three tickets to Elton John's Farewell Yellow Brick Road concert in Boston, in early November. I was so anxious to attend that concert that I hatched a plan.

"Do you suppose," I asked the surgeon, "that you could possibly schedule me for surgery the day after the concert? So I wouldn't have to miss it?"

"Excuse me," the doctor said, clearing his throat, "patients cannot request specific dates. And I only have use of the operating theatre for this surgery on the first Wednesday of the month."

That was when his assistant, who'd been consulting the calendar on his phone, announced, with a smile, that the first Wednesday of November was the day after the concert.

I was going to see Elton John perform, and be cured of cancer, all in the space of 12 hours!

October that year was no longer than any other October, but it felt as if it were. Finally it dragged to a close, and we were heading for Boston.

Five years later, and one tonsil down, I was still squamous-cell-cancer-free. However, in the meantime, this other issue had emerged.

At one of my six-month check-ups, the head and neck surgeon spotted a new, completely unrelated, cancer.

But his first thought was that it wasn't unrelated. "This is very uncommon," he said, but you have another tumor in your throat, behind the remaining tonsil. It looks like you have a second case of HPV-related cancer. I'm so sorry, Kate."

I had a clear memory of the long and painful recovery from that surgery, and I had no desire to go through it again, but it was looking as though I would have no choice.

"Am I allowed to say 'shit?'" I asked.

"Sure," he replied.

"SHIT!"

As it turned out, I was not facing a repetition of the previous cancer. Part of the tumor in my throat was removed and biopsied, and there it was, clear as day on the microscope slide: mantle cell lymphoma.

But I had survived my first bout of cancer with flying colors and I fully intended to do the same again.

A few weeks after my lymphoma diagnosis, I started three months of chemotherapy, administered over three days each month, followed by another three months of a different chemo cocktail every three weeks. After a month's break, I would have stem cells extracted from my bloodstream. The purpose of the preliminary infusions was to put me into remission so that those cells would be as healthy as possible when they were replaced in my bloodstream a week later.

In addition, because I would be receiving massive doses of chemotherapy throughout that intervening week, my transplanted stem cells would be doing their good work in a body that was cancer free—the grand plan being that it would remain cancer free.

Both of my cancer experiences were on my mind on T-Day Minus Nine, as I strolled around the congested streets of Boston, on my way back to Dana Farber. There was a good chance that I would one day be able to boast of being a "two-time cancer survivor"— thanks to my vastly experienced, incredibly gifted physicians.

I have already mentioned the outstanding reputation of my MEE surgeon; my Dana Farber oncologist was equally distinguished, heading up a team that focused almost exclusively on non-Hodgkins lymphoma. He'd be working closely with a second oncologist who would manage my chemotherapy in my local cancer center. To be treated by just one of these remarkable men would be a blessing; to have all three of them on my team was nothing short of miraculous.

It was rush hour, and I was held up briefly by a pick-up truck attempting to exit a parking garage into heavy traffic. When it was finally able to move off, the man in the passenger seat leaned out the window and said, "Sorry about that, sir."

Well, excuse me! I may be bald, but I still have boobs.

After my long day of conscious and unconscious preparation for the weeks ahead, Michael collected me and we drove back to the hotel, then ordered an Italian take-out from across the street. Ernie had a taste of it and smelled of garlic all the next day.

Chapter Seven: T-Day Minus Eight
Harvest Time

This was the day my dingle-dangles were scheduled to go to work for the first time. I arrived early at the Kraft Family Blood Donor Center at DFCI, Boston, and announced myself to the receptionist. I noticed that she had a rather furtive expression on her face when she heard my name, and, as I took my seat in the waiting area, I could hear her on the phone. "Kate Atkinson is here," she said. "Are you coming out or should I tell her?"

Tell me what?

A nurse emerged from the treatment room, to escort me through, I assumed, so I stood up and started to gather my belongings. But she gestured for me to sit down again.

"Ms. Atkinson," she began, with the expression on her face looking a lot like the receptionist's. "We're not quite ready to take you through because we're waiting for a call from Dr. Foster."

She went on to explain that my stem cell count was very low, possibly too low to make harvesting worthwhile. "If you don't mind waiting a little longer, Dr. Foster and his team have all the information. He'll let me know what he decides."

I felt a chill go through my body. After all the preparation—both physical and mental—all those months of chemotherapy, all the nausea, and bone pain, and sleepless nights; after giving up the work I loved, putting my life on hold, placing myself in the hands of the only people who could make me well, I was now hearing that it might not happen after all.

I couldn't bear the thought that it had all been in vain.

I had a bed waiting for me, and a nurse assigned to me. A breakfast tray had already been delivered, and my lunch had been ordered. All that remained was for me to take off my shoes, climb onto my bed and get hooked up. And all we needed to make that possible was a bumper crop of stem cells.

Thankfully, Sandy, my nurse, wasn't one just to hang around. She could see how distressed the news had made me and she sprang into action. Blood counts be damned, she was going to put me on that bed and get started. Sandy took every possible step she could without actually turning on the harvester (not combine). I did my best to wait patiently. With fearful thoughts spinning around in my brain, patience did not come easily.

After what seemed like hours but was probably twenty minutes, Sandy was called to the phone. She took the call with her back to me, but I could hear her end of the conversation.

"Uh huh, uh huh, yes… okay. Thank you." She hung up the phone and turned around.

Sandy's face was practically split in two by the world's biggest grin. She gave me two energetic thumbs up.

"We're on!" she exclaimed and flipped the switch with a flourish.

The harvesting process was a miracle of medical technology. All I had to do was lie there while blood flowed out one of the dingles in my chest tube and into the mother of all salad spinners. My stem cells were extracted, along with a similar number of red blood cells—because the machine can't tell the difference. They were collected in a baggie (medical term), while the rest of the blood went back into my vein through one of the dangles. The wonders of modern science!

Eventually, lunchtime rolled around: tuna salad sandwich, chips, mixed fruit, a cookie, and a can of ginger ale. Sandy had ordered it without knowing what I would like, and she got it nearly spot on. The only thing I didn't want was the ginger ale, because it was sugary, but I ate nearly everything else—and saved the chips for Michael.

My mother had a wondrous philosophy that airplane food has no calories. I, too, subscribed to that notion—and have extended it to encompass any food that arrives on a tray, including hospital food. It was not the caloric value of the soda that put me off; it was the taste. I am a voting member of the Diet Coke fan club. As for potato chips, well, Michael liked them more than I do, and he deserved a treat.

Each harvesting session lasted around five hours, at the end of which the baggie was delivered to some laboratory egghead responsible for separating the stem cells from the extraneous red blood cells, counting them—presumably using something other than an abacus—and reporting the total back to my Nurse Navigator. I'm not sure what was done with the rejected red blood cells; I hope they made their way to some poor anemic soul who needed them more than I did.

My Dana Farber oncologist was the brains behind the operation; Terry, my Nurse Navigator, was the brawn. She kept track of my appointment schedules, and made sure I knew where and when the appointments were. She provided orientation, and education about post- transplant care.

She also answered important questions like "Can I pet my puppy after the transplant?" Her answer was, "Yes, as long as you wash your hands afterwards and don't let him bite you or lick your face."

At the end of a stem cell harvest day, Terry would receive the count, and pass it on to the medical team and the harvestee (me). If an insufficient number of cells had been harvested (the minimum is two million across two days), she would arrange for a plerixafor injection. I'm sure she did a lot of other things, too, but in my case, these were the most important.

Terry called me late that Tuesday afternoon to report the stem cell count from the day's harvest, and the news was not good: the total for the day was only .86 million of the little rascals. Houston, we had a problem, because it would be no easy feat harvesting over a million more cells on day two.

I was scheduled for a second plerixafor injection that evening, and numerous fingers were crossed: my own and Michael's, to be sure, but also Terry's, Sandy's, Dr. Foster's and those of his team. Maybe even the laboratory egghead was rooting for me. And, if he'd had fingers to cross, I'm sure Ernie would have done so, too.

At the end of the day, Michael came to pick me up, and this time he brought Ernie with him. It was a good thing I didn't have to worry about face-licking yet! Not for the first time I found myself wondering how Ernie and I were going to manage being apart for three weeks.

When we reached the hotel, Michael dropped off Ernie and me while he went to park the car and scout out a restaurant for our take-out dinner. He gave me the room key card, and Ernie and I took the elevator to our floor.

Then what?

I checked the key card; of course there was no number on it. That was written on the paper wallet next to the television in our room. But where was our room? Ernie and I walked up and down every corridor, while I surreptitiously waved the key card at any promising looking door, to no avail.

Ernie was a good boy; he only barked once—at a half-empty bottle of red wine someone had left outside their room. Frankly, by that stage, I'm surprised that I didn't bark at the bottle... or take a swig from it.

We gave up looking. When Michael arrived, he found Ernie and me waiting forlornly by the elevator. Michael clearly found it amusing that I was unable to find our room, but I reminded him that I'd barely been there, while he was in and out of it numerous times during the day.

A few steps later we arrived at our door. It was right next to the room with the half-empty wine bottle. Ernie hadn't been barking at the bottle; he was telling me we'd found our room!

Take-out that night was from a Thai restaurant. To celebrate my last night of liberty for who knew how long, Michael poured Diet Coke into a martini glass for me. "Here's to freedom," we said, raising our glasses, meaning the treatment that would give me back mine.

Ernie, still looking smug for having pointed out our room earlier, posed with me for a photograph. There we were: an adorable pup, with a little old bald lady holding a martini glass full of Diet Coke, and with the serene look of enough faith to move mountains.

Chapter Eight: T-Day Minus Seven
Poor Candidate

Without that sustaining faith, I doubt I would have had the strength to face this challenge. And I might not have relied so heavily on that faith if it weren't for some events that occurred thirty years earlier.

Before I entered the priesthood—or even suspected that was where I was headed—I ran, with a staff of seven, the mail order division of an environmental non-profit. For most of my eight years with the organization, I had loved my job.

After those eight enjoyable years, however, I started to feel dissatisfied—while, at the same time, becoming more and more involved with my church. At the request of the rector, I taught Sunday School, served on committees, led prayers and read scripture in worship services, even preached on occasion. I assumed the rector thought that, as a single woman, I had lots of free time.

Little did I know my rector had something far more significant on his mind.

As I took on the increasing number of parish duties, I wondered how I might reduce my day job hours and increase my more fulfilling time spent at church.

One Monday morning, I was summoned to a meeting with the HR Director and the Director of Fundraising. Before anyone even spoke, I knew what was about to happen, and silently, I rejoiced.

I was right. My directors informed me that, in a cost-cutting exercise, the mail order operation was going to be moved to an external fulfillment house. My staff and I were all being laid off.

I could barely contain my delight! Now I could re-order my life priorities, while leaving my job with a good-sized severance payment in my pocket.

Careful not to let my superiors see how overjoyed the news had made me, I agreed that their decision was both sensible and cost-effective. They were so surprised by my calm demeanor that they granted my request to remain in the office while they gave the news to each of the other members of my team.

Some of the younger ones cried, and certainly there was shock; no one else had seen this coming. But somehow, my composure had a positive effect on my team. After we'd all received the news, I gathered us into a meeting room. We sat around the table, and I invited everyone to take hands in a circle. We didn't pray—it wasn't church, after all—but our care and affection for one another was palpable; it gave us strength, and hope for the future. Less than two weeks later, all seven of those team members had found new jobs.

I decided to create my own job. I set myself up as a marketing consultant and copywriter—to ensure that I had a regular income—and used my newly increased spare time to take on more parish duties. This continued, to my immense satisfaction, for several months.

One day my rector, Father Mark, came to see me.

As we sat at the dining room table, drinking tea and chatting, he suddenly leaned forward and said, "You do realize that God is calling you to ordained ministry, don't you? So, what are you going to do about it?"

The moment he spoke, the room filled with light—as though the sun had burst out from behind a cloud.

Except that it hadn't. It was the first time in my life that I'd experienced a vision, and I knew, in that instant, with utter clarity, that Father Mark was right.

God doesn't always show up in wondrous ways—like a room filling with light. God also speaks to us through disgruntlement, disappointment, and loss. God uses the full range of human emotions to get a point across. If I had not been laid off from my secular job, I might never have become a priest.

And if one vision has done the trick, God is not going to waste time handing out another one. A few months after my rector's visit, when I had started the process of seeking ordination, I took a night class on the New Testament, at a local college, with my friend, Alicia. One evening, we drove there together and parked next door at the Anglican Cathedral.

As I waited for Alicia to lock her car, I glanced up at the top of the cathedral where, instead of a cross, there was a gilded angel. In front of my very eyes, the angel turned in my direction and lowered her right arm as if in blessing. Could God be speaking to me again by bringing a statue to life? Struck dumb, I began to claw at Alicia's elbow and point upwards.

"Oh," she said, calmly, "I didn't know the arm moved, too."

Unbeknownst to me, the angel was a weathervane!

Now, thirty years later, I arrived for the second time at the Blood Center, where my zero-calorie breakfast tray waited for me.

Along with some bad news.

Because the total number of stem cells collected on the first day had been significantly less than ideal, and because it's unusual for the second day's collection to be greater than the first day's, my care team expressed deep concern. Two million cells is the absolute minimum requirement; the optimal number across two days is three million. With only .86 million cells to show for Tuesday's harvest, I looked like a poor candidate for an autologous transplant—the re-introduction of one's own stem cells after they have been removed and stripped of every last vestige of cancer. Or, as I prefer to describe the process, laundered.

It was unsettling to discover I was likely a "poor candidate." More than unsettling—devastating, a real blow to my confidence and self-esteem. But in this case being a poor candidate also put me in a life-or-death situation. Would I, or would I not, have enough retrievable stem cells to make a transplant viable?

When Sandy hooked me up to the salad spinner, my head was spinning, too. What if my body wouldn't cooperate? Would I be "laid off" and sent home? Would we have to seek alternative, less successful treatments? We were all on tenterhooks—not just my husband and I, but Sandy, Terry, my oncologist... the whole transplant team.

I was scheduled to be admitted to BWH that evening, for the next phase of my treatment, but that next phase was now in doubt. While my blood flowed down one line and back another, and the harvester did its work, my mind kept going to dark places.

Finally, a decision was made.

"Dr. Foster called," Sandy announced. "He said that if we don't meet the stem cell quota today, you should stay in Boston for another night, and come back tomorrow morning for a third collection."

It was a good plan, and it lessened my anxiety somewhat, but it also introduced a new worry. We had left our cat, Charlie, at home with a clean litter box and enough food for three nights. Would adding another night mean that he ran out of food and clean litter?

And then came the final answer. This time Dr. Foster himself appeared at my bedside.

"We've decided to admit you to the hospital tonight, just as we'd planned," he reassured me. "But if your stem cell count should happen to... fall short... you won't have to leave. We'll arrange for a third collection."

And Michael could go home and feed Charlie.

My bed wouldn't be ready for me until that evening, so, when my collection session was over, and the baggie was on its merry way to the lab, Michael, Ernie, and I went for a walk in between the medical buildings and found a small shopping center with a seating area. Terry would be contacting us as soon as she had the count for the day, so we hung out for a couple of hours, there in the food hall, waiting for that all-important phone call...

And then it came. Terry's voice sounded jubilant: "We collected 1.6 million stem cells today... that makes a total of nearly 2.5 million!"

I was not a poor candidate after all; I was on my way to being cured!

Chapter Nine: T-Day Minus Six
Nobody is an Island

After I received the life-changing news, that I was a viable transplant candidate after all, I had to begin the painful process of saying goodbye—not so much to Michael; after all, he would be visiting me over the next three weeks. He would be calling me every day.

But it broke my heart to be parted from my puppy.

Ernie is a mama's boy and has been from the moment he arrived.

Ever since I was given my first kitten, when I was eight years old, I have been a cat person. A year before my lymphoma diagnosis, I had lost my beloved old lady cat, Surrey, who lived to be 18 years old. She had seen me through some of the most difficult times in my life—including my first bout with cancer, when she lay beside me while I struggled with outrageous post-surgery pain, and welcomed the effects of pain meds that didn't come often enough. She was my comforter when my mother and father died just four months apart. She was my companion when Michael had to work away from home for nearly three challenging years. And when Alex's adolescence arrived with a vengeance, Surrey was a steadfast, soothing presence. I adored her. I was heartbroken when we realized it was time to let her go.

Our second cat, Charlie, was ten years younger than Surrey, and the bane of her existence. He enjoyed nothing more than to hide around corners and jump on her when she walked by. This became increasingly upsetting to Surrey as the arthritis in her hips progressed, but Charlie persisted. He explained to us (in a language any pet-lover will understand) that she liked it. He, too, missed her when she died.

Michael and I liked having two pets, but we agreed that we didn't want to get another cat. Surrey was unique; we knew we'd be unable to stop ourselves making comparisons. It wouldn't be fair to the poor, unsuspecting new cat.

Six years previously, my sister Joanie—who, like me, had always been a cat person—suddenly adopted an adorable, lop-eared pup, whom she named Brenda. They became inseparable, the best of friends. Brenda has enriched her mom's life in countless ways.

I had always said that I would never have a dog, but I found myself thinking, "If Joanie can do it, maybe we could, too."

One Saturday morning, while Michael and I were drinking coffee in bed, and using our laptops, I asked Google a question. "What is a good dog for people who have only ever had cats?"

And, of course, Google knew the answer. It listed several breeds, but the one that caught my eye was Cavalier King Charles Spaniel. While Michael was innocently looking up the news of the day, I was not-so-innocently looking up breeders. And I found one. I was presented with a screen full of boxes, each containing the face of a Cavalier puppy. Slightly off center and down to the left, was a rust-colored cutie with a smudge of white on his nose and chin. The name under his box was Elijah.

All the puppies were adorable, but I kept going back to Elijah, with his non-symmetrical markings and his black button nose. Before I knew it, I was quietly completing the online application, and, when I was nearly finished, I turned to Michael and informed him that I was about to click on a major purchase. But, oh, such a lovable one! Did I have his permission?

Michael wins the prize in the understanding husband category. He knew I was heartbroken over losing Surrey, and he wanted nothing more than to heal my sorrow—even if it meant taking out a line of credit (which it did).

"Let's do it," he said, and, with Michael's hand over mine, we clicked on Elijah, and he was ours.

Then we changed his name to Ernie.

Coincidentally, Ernie arrived on my 65th birthday— a little ball of fur with a non-stop tongue. From the moment we met, he seemed to understand that his purpose in life was to love his mum. He stormed my heart, and—just like Joanie and Brenda—we became inseparable. Who knew I was a dog person?

But now, during my hospitalization, Ernie and I were going to be separated for three weeks.

When I woke up in my hospital room on T-Day-6, there was no little buddy leaping on the bed to say good morning. When Michael called, he told me that Ernie had, as usual, scampered up the stairs after his morning pee, and was distressed to find me missing. He loves Michael, too—especially since Michael is in charge of pet-feeding—yet Ernie is quite clear on the subject: "There's nobody," he says, "quite like my Mum."

But I had work to do. Being cured of cancer is a group effort and I had a major part to play.

Twice daily, for six days, I would receive mega doses of chemicals designed to kill off any surviving trace of lymphoma. The unfortunate side effect was that they would also kill off my immune system, leaving me susceptible to... well, to just about any germ that managed to reach me.

My accommodations were designed to prevent germs from reaching me. There was a constant, and very noisy, air exchange system. The door to the room was vacuum-sealed, which made it difficult to open, especially when my strength started to drain away. Anyone who entered the room had to wear a mask and gloves, and I, too, had to be masked whenever someone else was present. Not when I was alone though, thank goodness.

Apparently, my accommodations were also designed to prevent residents from getting too attached because the primary aim is to send patients home, freeing up beds for the next ones. My room was spartan: bed, recliner, window seat, IV stand, commode, TV, and a minuscule bathroom. The one luxury item was a small fridge, which I promptly filled with Diet Coke and pudding cups. I was on the sixth floor, which meant that I could at least see a slice of sky in between the medical buildings.

The heliport was right above me, and I could hear helicopters arriving and departing almost daily. As I listened to their clatter, I realized that the sound of a medical helicopter is unlike any other. Perhaps it's because they were flying so close—but also because of their purpose. One way or another, medical helicopters are almost always engaged in saving lives. They might be transporting a patient from the scene of a catastrophic accident, or from one hospital to another, better equipped institution. They might be collecting or delivering organs for transplant, ensuring that a lost life could give life to someone else.

I rarely saw the helicopters, although I often saw their shadows moving across the face of a building. But hearing them always made me stop and think, whose life hung in the balance on this trip? What had happened? Were there others involved, anxiously awaiting news, or trying desperately to reach their loved one's bedside? Or, were there family members, newly bereaved, finding comfort in knowing their dear departed was an organ donor? So many stories, with so many lives involved each time a helicopter flew in.

My forced retirement, combined with the reduction in my activity level, gave me time and space to be philosophical. My medical helicopter musings reflected the theme of human connections, not a new one for me.

When he was ill, poet John Donne wrote a meditation now remembered most for its first line, "No man is an island." To paraphrase it: we are all attached to a land mass of family, friends, and animals. The closer we are to those fellow human beings and cherished pets, the more we are affected by developments in each other's life.

One of the first things I did after being admitted to BWH, was to set up a text group with half a dozen college friends.

We instantly lit up the air waves!

As I sat in my recliner, with my first bag of poison dripping into my vein, my phone dinged constantly with messages of love, good vibes, and encouragement.

"You've got this, Kate. We're all pulling for you."
Those six friends were a fraction of the circle I was blessed to inhabit. I may have moved into my hospital room alone, but I was accompanied in the hearts of dozens of people I love, supporting me on my journey.

And Ernie would be waiting for me when the day came for me to go home again.

Chapter Ten: T-Day Minus Five
A Cast of Characters

It was time to get to know my new circle, the nurses, nursing assistants, doctors, and support staff who would be caring for me over the next three weeks. I would form a special bond with these people, while we worked together toward our common goal: making me well again. That bond had already been forged with Sandy in the blood donor center, and I called her to make sure she had heard the good news about my stem cell count.

"Yes," she said, "and I'm thrilled for you!"

Florence, the nurse assigned to me that first day, was in and out of my room a lot—and she liked to talk. She had been in nursing for over 30 years, and she really knew her stuff—in fact she frequently second guessed the doctors. I could ask her about anything: what was happening to me, when would my hair grow back, and how would Michael and I manage once I was home again?

I could ask general questions about my treatment too. You name it, Florence had an answer. In our fascinating conversations, I always learned at least one new thing. For example, she told me that because of our heavy-duty chemo blasts, most transplant patients have digestive system issues. Loss of appetite is common.

"But," Florence confided, "nearly everybody craves ramen noodles."

I decided to reserve judgment, especially as I still had some appetite.

I met part of my doctor team that first day too, a jolly, round woman, Dr. Chen, whose smile filled her entire face, and remained in place even when she was talking about such unpleasant things as hives or diarrhea.

Dr. Chen was accompanied by an intern, Dr. Miller, who could not have been more different in appearance, or personality, from her supervisor. Tall, willowy, and oh so solemn, Dr. Miller took her job very seriously. It was enough to make me spring to attention when she placed her stethoscope on my back and told me to take deep breaths.

Dr. Miller outlined, very carefully and sternly, my schedule of chemo treatments over the next six days. I was afraid to tell her that Florence had already done that. Besides, I had a print-out I could refer to—in case I wanted to know whether it was the cytarabine or the melphalan that was making me crave ramen noodles.

It is common practice for one's nurse to be present during the physicians' visits, but I had a feeling that Florence would have been present whether or not it was expected. After the doctors had left that morning, she ran through my chemo schedule for the third time, and made a couple of corrections to Dr. Miller's spiel.

As the days went by, and Florence was assigned to me nearly every time she was on duty, I soon discovered that she had plenty to say about subjects other than cancer treatment. Mainly about other people.

Florence complained that the neighbor on one side of her house was having an extension built—which, in her view, was too large, and too inappropriate.

Neighbors on the other side had a tree that annoyingly shed its leaves in her backyard, so, when she took her dog out to pee, she just happened to make sure he peed on their grass. Her neighbors across the street must be spies, Florence assured me, because they keep changing their front door light bulb to different colors that had nothing to do with the seasons. Clearly an espionage signal! And she absolutely knew that the neighbor two houses down had stolen some lumber from the construction site next door, so she rang his doorbell and told him to put it back. He did... but only some of it.

How did she know? She was watching, probably from behind a twitching curtain.

With so much time spent monitoring her neighbors' movements, it was a wonder to me that Florence could fit nursing into her schedule.

Not surprisingly, Florence had observations on people and procedures at BWH in general, and on our floor specifically. She was in and out of my room more and more frequently, not necessarily because there were tasks she needed to perform, but because she was staying to chat.

This was fine with me as long our conversations dealt with topics such as my blood counts or digestive system. Yet, increasingly, I heard her criticize fellow nurses, past and present, various doctors, and even other patients.

To her credit, Florence never breached HIPAA (the Health Insurance Portability and Accountability Act), which protects the privacy of patients, but she often rolled her eyes and said, "I know which room I'd rather be in," when called to another of her patients.

Sometimes I thought, "If she talks to me about other people like this, what's she saying about me to them?" But mostly I was happy to have those mainly one-sided conversations with her. I enjoyed her company.

Most important, Florence took excellent care of me and seemingly knew all there was to know about my specific condition.

A small group of "regulars," comprised of RNs, care assistants, and a handful of other staff members also contributed to my care. Others were called in periodically from other departments, because BWH, like so many hospitals, was experiencing a shortage of nurses and LNAs (Licensed Nursing Assistants). COVID-19 had such a disastrous effect on medical personnel across the board, that I wonder if we will ever recover. But there is hope in our younger generations!

For several nights, a young, newly licensed RN, Bonnie, was on the floor, shadowing a more experienced nurse. I was struck by how carefully and earnestly Bonnie approached every task. When I was receiving a medication that she had to administer intravenously, over the course of two minutes, she repeatedly turned her head to check the wall clock, making sure she injected the medicine, as directed, into my IV line.

When she'd finished, I couldn't stop myself channeling my charmingly outspoken mother. "The day will come, Bonnie," I said, "when you won't need to look at the clock, because you'll have a sense when two minutes have passed. But you'll check it anyway."

"You're going to be a very good nurse," I continued, "because you pay attention, ask questions, and never assume you know everything there is to know."

Another twenty-something, Violet, who had only a little more experience than Bonnie, arrived for the night shift at 6:00 PM. When we met for the first time, she had something complicated to do with my IV set-up, and she was in my room for a while.

As usual, I was being my jokey self, and I don't think she was used to that, coming from an old lady with cancer. Her response, every time I made her laugh, was, "You're so cute!"

Her observation sent me off on more philosophical musing.

"You know, Violet," I observed, "from the day we're born, until around age ten, we're told how cute we are, but it trails off after that, for around … fifty years."

She laughed.

"Then one has the prospect of becoming cute again," I added.

Apparently, at least in Violet's eyes, I was a cute little old lady—because I made her laugh.

The Patient Care Assistants (PCAs) were a mixed group. Half of them were career LNAs, such as Roland, one of the night staff, who always had a project going on in his yard—bird feeders, solar lights, or new flowering plants. I heard all about those projects while he took my vital signs at 6:00 AM.

Another PCA, Diane, worked days, and she and I sang together when she came into my room. Two favorites were *Somewhere Over the Rainbow* and *Here Comes the Sun*. One morning, Diane and I sang *What's New, Pussycat?* I must have overdone it on the "Whoa-ohs," because a doctor burst into the room to make sure everything was alright!

The other group of PCAs was composed of nursing students receiving practical experience as part of their training, or who were earning money to pay for their schooling. I admit to channeling my mother with them, too—although I stopped myself from yelling, "Say, 'You're welcome!'" to Holly, who, whenever I thanked her, always replied, "No problem."

It was gratifying to see young people embracing nursing as a career. And not just nursing, but cancer nursing. According to a recent public service commercial on TV, one in four people will develop cancer in their   lifetime. My experience tells me that it takes a special breed of person to care for that 25%.

I had firsthand experience of that special breed before I even arrived in Boston, when I was receiving monthly chemotherapy treatments at my local cancer center. The treatment area was a long room with ten recliners set at intervals against a wall with windows, and three more recliners against the facing wall, which was dominated by a multi-station computer desk. The nurses sat there when they weren't tending to patients. They didn't sit very much.

Whenever I could, I would take one of the recliners on the desk side of the room. I chose those seats so I could look out a window, but they also gave me a good view of the other patients, and the nurses caring for them.

Having cancer doesn't usually change a person's personality—although it might amplify existing traits. The treatment room was nearly always full, and was   populated by all kinds, a microcosm of the world in general: angry folks, whiny folks, sweet folks, and timid folks. Some folks who didn't speak English. There were people who brought their laptops so that they could do their jobs without interruption. Others insisted on chatting to the person in the neighboring chair, even if that person would obviously rather be left alone. Introverts, extroverts, prima donnas, grouches, weepers, gentlemen and ladies, and of course, jokers—and I was one of those.

Through it all, the nurses remained calm, gentle, and kind. And however politely (or not) a need was expressed, it was met instantly—from a warm blanket to an extra pillow, to a cold drink. Nothing was too much; their patience was limitless. As I have often said, cancer nurses are angels.

Of course, they are also human beings. It would not surprise me to learn that the angels who ministered to us so patiently, sometimes went home and yelled at their partners. Or, like Florence, vented their frustrations to someone else willing to listen.

For the most part, when I was still rector of my parish, I strived to be a "non-anxious presence." Parishioners could talk to me about anything (and did) without fear of shocking me or of being judged. Listening, really listening, is one of the most important aspects of ministry, and it usually means seeing beyond personality traits to the heart of the individual. Nursing is like that too.

Did I go home and yell at my husband from time to time? Of course I did!

Along with the doctors, nurses, and care assistants at BWH, there was a vast number of support staff, without whom the place would have fallen apart. Two stand out in my mind.

Daisy, a cleaner, came into my room every morning, clutching a bouquet of trash bags she had carefully prepared by tying a knot in each one, so they would fit the large wastebaskets. The more loudly and cheerfully I bellowed, "Good morning!" to Daisy, she always topped me. And then I would ask her how she was, and she would sing out, "I'm GOOD!" Daisy's clothes were threadbare, and her shoes were decidedly down at the heels. It wouldn't surprise me to learn that Daisy's life beyond BWH was sparse— but you'd never have known it from her attitude.

I never caught the name of the other cleaner who came by every day. He was like a timid little mouse, knocking gently on the door and practically tiptoeing in to change the trash bag in the bathroom. I knew better than to try to have cheerful greeting competitions with him, the way I did with Daisy, but I did get as far as finding out if he were having a good day. He always was.

From the observations Florence, shared with me, I knew she was highly attuned to other people's failings, and quick to criticize. I was, therefore, surprised to discover that she had introduced a recognition scheme for the staff. Florence was the only judge. She awarded the prize, which was a little bag containing a starfish pin and a card printed with the following:

The Starfish Story by Loren Eiseley

One day a man was walking along the beach when he noticed a boy picking up and gently throwing things into the ocean.

Approaching the boy he asked, "Young man, what are you doing?"

"Throwing starfish back into the ocean. The surf is up and the tide is going out. If I don't throw them back, they'll die," the boy replied.

The man laughed to himself and said, "Do you realize there are miles and miles of beach and hundreds of starfish? You can't make any difference."

After listening politely, the boy bent down to pick up another starfish and threw it into the surf. Then he smiled at the man and said, "I made a difference to that one."

Florence awarded her little prizes to staff members who had made a difference, not necessarily through medical expertise, but through connection; through awareness of people's needs; through generosity with time, and a listening ear... basically, by leaving a space a little better, a little happier, than when they entered it.

As for judging a book by its cover, Florence had plenty of inner pages that were not very nice! But she also had pages full of kindness, non-critical awareness, and the belief that recognizing a positive presence goes a long way to ensure that presence continues.

I don't know who Florence has given a starfish pin to, but, in my experience at BWH, many deserved one. And Florence saw it, too.

Chapter Eleven: T-Day Minus Four
Please Don't Let Me Die

At 2:00 in the morning, I had what was possibly the most frightening experience of my life.

I was awakened by Violet coming in to hang a new IV baggie, and I took that opportunity to visit the bathroom. When I came back to bed, my head started buzzing in a way I'd never experienced before.

"Does this chemo make you feel weird?" I asked Violet.

"I don't think so," she answered. "But what do you mean by 'weird?'"

By that time, I was holding my head in my hands and the room was spinning. As Violet helped me lie back on the bed, my vision turned into a long tunnel.

"I'm losing consciousness," I told her.

The next thing I knew, the room was full of nurses, my johnny coat was being pulled open to expose my chest, and a blood pressure cuff was being strapped on my arm. I could hear the nurses' voices fading in and out, but I couldn't open my eyes, and I couldn't move.

"I can hear you," I said, and my voice sounded reedy in my ears. I can't say that my life flashed before my eyes, but I was terrified that it was ending.

Violet told me to squeeze her hand, which I did. Her hand became my lifeline.

"Please don't let me die," I pleaded in my thin little voice.

Then, everything changed. Even before the doctor arrived, I opened my eyes and said, still shakily, "I'm okay now." The relief on the nurses' faces was palpable.

Someone kindly covered up my bare chest, and I noticed there was a lot of fumbling going on in the corner. It turned out there were two sets of heart monitor wires in the room, one of which—the one that was connected to my monitor—had fallen behind the bed. Not realizing this, two nurses were attempting to attach the other set to my chest, but it was not showing any data on the monitor—not because I had died, but because it was not connected!

The third nurse, Violet, was still holding my hand, and I whispered to her, "The Three Stooges!" She suppressed her giggle admirably and whispered back, "You're cute!"

Once the heart monitor conundrum had been remedied, I sat up on the side of the bed. I assume there was still some worry about the possibility I'd had a stroke, because Violet asked me if I knew her name and could tell her where I was. "Yes," I replied. "Your name is Violet and I'm in Timbuktu!" Then someone asked if I knew the date, and I admit I cheated a little on that one, glancing at the whiteboard where useful information was written daily.

That's when I spotted my blood pressure—which had been noted in dry marker when I was in the throes of my episode: 193/104. Yikes! But it had returned to normal by that time, plus the heart monitor was showing nice, even beats.

When the doctor arrived, there was nothing for her to do. I was conscious, alert, aware of my surroundings, and feeling bad that we had probably awakened her from a nap. She agreed with my layperson's diagnosis that I'd been "fighting a faint." My body had been trying to lose consciousness, but I wouldn't let it, because I was afraid I was dying.

When everything had settled down, and I was alone again, I couldn't sleep. I think I may have been suffering from a touch of PTSD, because my mind kept going back to that awful feeling of helplessness and mortality. It was nearly 3:00 in the morning, and I wanted nothing more than to call Robyn, my best friend, and hear her comforting voice.

Robyn and I had met in our sophomore year at high school, when she was the new girl. We were in a brand new building, where some trusting architect had made the decision to provide open cubbies for a bunch of   teenagers, instead of lockers. The bank of cubbies was arranged in five rows, from floor level to around seven feet high, in alphabetical order by last name, top to bottom. Because Robyn's last name was higher up in the alphabet, so was her cubby, immediately above mine. The problem was that Robyn was only 5'3" and could barely reach it. I once saw her trying to take down some heavy books and I was afraid they were going to fall on her head.

I was four inches taller than Robyn, so I offered to switch cubbies with her. She readily agreed, and we became fast friends from that moment on.

Fifteen-year-olds are a breed all their own. Robyn and I spent the year collecting LPs and that modern invention, audio cassettes, of new artists we were discovering daily: Cat Stevens, James Taylor, Joni Mitchell, Elton John... all great performers who still haven't lost their appeal, more than fifty years later. And as well as being music-mad, we were boy-crazy.

In those days, life was all about first forays of all kinds. Robyn and I have been through much together. We went on to the same college; we dated together; we were at each other's weddings—although Robyn beat me to marriage by ten years; we both miscarried and ended up with only children—Graham in her case, Alex in mine; our mothers both died of cancer in the same year, and our fathers both developed Alzheimers disease. We have traveled together, studied together, taken risks together, dieted together, and drunk too much together. We have wept together, and oh, how we have laughed!

And here we were, more than 50 years later, still the best of friends.

For much of the time we've known each other, Robyn and I have lived thousands of miles apart, but we have always been at the end of each other's phone.

At 3:00 AM, in my lonely hospital room, all I wanted to do was to call my dearest friend and tell her how I was feeling. She would have understood.

I didn't call her. Eventually, I fell asleep again. The terror I had experienced during the night faded away when the morning sunlight filled my room.

But I still called Robyn as soon as it was a decent time to do so.

What had caused that traumatic event? Dr. Chen and her solemn sidekick told me, on morning rounds, that I had experienced a "vasovagal episode," a fancy term for fainting. It was likely related to my chemotherapy. They would not be altering my treatment, I was glad to hear, but they would be starting me on medication for hypertension, to control my wildly fluctuating blood pressure.

After my college friends received my group text describing what had happened to me, they all sent sympathetic messages. Also a flurry of texts suggesting that I get myself a helmet to wear when I go to the bathroom in the middle of the night. My friend, Paula, even attached an image of what it should look like: a Viking helmet, with horns.

I must have been feeling better, because I wrote back:

"I love the helmet. Not only will it protect my head, but if anyone annoys me, I can charge them like a bull and gore 'em!"

Chapter Twelve: T-Day Minus Three
Bone-Breaking and Leave-Taking

Six weeks before going to Boston, I'd completed my first rounds of chemotherapy, and Michael and I had been looking forward to enjoying a month of "living large," in the words of my oncologist. We had arranged four get-aways during April, beginning with two nights at a hotel in the Lakes Region of New Hampshire.

The night before we were due to leave, I came down with a gastric virus. We had to cancel. But we didn't mind too much because we could still enjoy the following week we'd booked in the White Mountains.

Because of my upset stomach, I didn't eat anything for two days, and my body was already weakened by cancer and chemotherapy. At the end of the second day, I was standing in the kitchen one minute, and the next I was flat on my back on the tile floor. I don't think I fainted; I just fell.

The next morning, I was in so much pain I could hardly move. We canceled our week in the White Mountains.

I paid a visit to the ER where they x-rayed me and found nothing wrong. At my follow-up appointment, however, the doctor told me it appeared I had broken some ribs. There's no treatment for that other than rest.

A week later, I returned to St. Cat's for a special service and celebration in honor of my retirement. The bishop was there to support me, but I was the preacher. The pews overflowed with beloved people—every one of whom wore a mask in order to keep me safe.

My sermon topic that Sunday morning was John's gospel account of Jesus entering a locked room after his crucifixion.

> *Jesus appeared to his disciples in his resurrected body. Imagine: this is a body unlike any other—a glorious, unfettered body; a body that can enter a locked room; that has the power to breathe the Holy Spirit. It's a body that could be the ultimate in perfection—and yet it isn't.*
>
> *Jesus' resurrected body carries the marks of crucifixion, of horrific, painful injury, of wounds inflicted by human beings—of wounds that are a direct result of his choice to live as a man in an imperfect world.*
>
> *Jesus' crucifixion wounds are the only man-made thing in heaven. What that says to me is that those wounds are vitally important. Why? Because they signify what is perhaps the most essential aspect of being human—and that is that we suffer. We human beings all suffer. It's what makes us human, and it's a major part of what made Jesus human.*

Ironically, throughout that service, I was suffering! I was in so much pain, I was afraid I'd be unable to continue.

But I did. I preached, I presided at Communion and then, completely unexpectedly, I sat on a specially provided seat while, one after another, parish Wardens, current and past, made presentations.

Michael, Alex, Joanie, and other speakers, gave their own tributes.

Afterwards, I was seated in another special chair, this time in the parish hall, while parishioners were invited, one by one, to share their farewells with me.

Michael and Alex were at my side, offering and receiving their own good wishes. The line of people stretched out of the room, guided by velvet ropes similar to those one might see in a theatre.

Downstairs, St. Cat's hospitality team had provided one of their famously delicious spreads. But I was too busy saying goodbye to take even a look! Alex went down to the reception and brought Michael and me egg salad on bridge rolls and deviled eggs, our favorites. We missed out, however, on Mary's famous salmon mousse.

I managed not to cry throughout the service and the reception line, but it was a different story at home, after I began reading the huge basketful of cards from my parishioners. Each card affected me more than the last one. Through my tears, I read of their gratitude for my touching lives, bringing comfort, helping with significant life changes, and praying from my heart.

The notes thanked me for presiding at weddings, baptisms, and funerals of loved ones, for being a part of life's milestones. Over and over again, my parishioners expressed heartfelt wishes for my full recovery and a blessed retirement.

These were my peeps, the people I had cared for and loved for over 13 years. Now they were loving and caring for me as I went through the toughest months of my life.

My older brother, Jim, who lives in Atlanta, the furthest away of my three siblings, made the trip to be there on my special day. Despite being brought up in a solidly Episcopalian household, Jim is not religious. He is gruff and taciturn, but the rest of us don't let him get away with it because we know he has a heart of gold.

He came to my leaving service, he joined in the hymns, and he listened to me preach. That's how Jimbo shows how much he loves his sister.

The next trip Michael and I had planned was a four-day visit with Robyn and her family, leaving that afternoon as soon as the parish celebrations were over. However, when we got home, I sat down in my chair, hurting so much that I couldn't get up again.

I called Robyn and canceled our visit. There went trip number three. I felt terrible for letting her down. But, with Robyn, there was no need to feel terrible because she understood.

"All I care about is your pain," Robyn assured me. "All I want is for you to get better."

The next day, I called my doctor's office and made an appointment. But the earliest they could get me in was the end of the week. By then I was finding it so hard to walk that Michael borrowed a wheelchair for me. He brought me to the waiting area and a nurse pushed me into the examination room.

When my doctor saw how incapacitated I was, she immediately had me admitted to the hospital, for pain control. She ordered an MRI. She even wheeled me to the ER herself.

My diagnosis? I had compression fractures in four vertebrae. I had been walking around with a broken back.

Three days of intravenous drugs later, I was well enough to be discharged—with pain meds, a back brace, and my trusty wheelchair. It was a good thing too, because our fourth, and last, April getaway was due to begin that afternoon.

To celebrate our wedding anniversary the next day, Michael had, months earlier, booked a surprise destination for a three-night stay. This was one trip I refused to cancel!

So, with me encased in my brace and propped up in the passenger's seat, and my lovely hubby at the wheel, off we went on our magical mystery tour. I fell asleep for the second half of the journey, and, when I opened my eyes, we had arrived. It was a hotel, near Mount Washington, that we had discovered the previous year, when Michael celebrated my birthday with a long weekend there.

We had fallen in love with this spot, and I was thrilled to be back again. We had two full days of relaxation and recreation—just what we needed after a challenging eight months.

Although my susceptibility to germs, coupled with my osteoporosis-diminished, broken bones had prevented us from enjoying the three other get-aways we'd planned to make the most of my month of "living large," I thoroughly enjoyed our anniversary treat. It would be a long time before we could travel again.

Then, just three days after returning home, we were on our way to Boston.

......

Shortly after arriving at BWH, I had been drinking a cup of tea while talking to our daughter Alex on the phone. When I burst out laughing at something Alex said, my tea went down the wrong way and I had a violent coughing fit.

The next day, when the medical team made their rounds, and Dr. Miller listened to my lungs, she ordered a CT scan of my chest. It turned out I had aspiration pneumonia, caused by inhaling the tea I had choked on the day before. Whoops!

Next thing I knew, I had an oxygen cannula up my nose, and a bag of antibiotics had been added to my IV stand.

I was already getting my chemo infusions twice a day. I was also receiving what seemed like gallons of saline fluid, because chemotherapy can, and did, affect the kidneys. My dingle-dangles were working overtime!

After the ward had been remodeled a few years earlier, the floors had settled, leaving them with a small incline. Because the IV stands were on wheels, they could roll across patients' rooms if they weren't properly wedged against something immobile—such as the end of the bed, or a wall.

My IV stand rolled across the floor so many times, that Violet decided it had a mind of its own. She christened it "Bernie." There may still be an IV stand on that floor, wearing a yellow sticky note that reads "My name is Bernie."

Violet also put a sticky note on the wall, in the corner of the room where I had my travel kettle, my single cup coffee maker, and a supply of coffee, tea, and sugar. She labeled that well-stocked corner, "Kate's Kitchen."

I had come to BWH prepared to brew my own coffee and tea, both very strong, the way I like them. I enjoyed several cups a day, along with a can or more of Diet Coke.

Drs. Miller and Chen had noticed that my ankles were swollen due to fluid retention—not a good problem to have when there is already extraneous fluid in one's lungs. They prescribed a powerful diuretic. Considering the combination of a nearly constant trickle of fluids into my veins, more Diet Coke than was good for me, multiple cups of strong coffee and tea, plus a no-nonsense diuretic, it's not difficult to conclude where I spent much of my time.

The night after my fainting episode, I woke up at around 1:30, needing to pee. I had never noticed before how spooky my room looked in the middle of the night—backlit here and there by dim nightlights, while Bernie rolled silently from one side of the room to the other. I realized that I was still traumatized by the previous night's events, because I felt reluctant to get up and go to the bathroom. So I just lay there, willing Bernie to stop moving before he yanked the IV out of my chest.

I did my best to ignore my full bladder, and waited for Violet to come and hang my 2:00 AM bag of saline solution.

After around 20 minutes, with Bernie finally at rest against the wastebasket, Violet came in. She'd already instructed me to get up slowly from a horizontal position—to avoid light-headedness—so I gradually hauled myself up until I was seated on the edge of the bed.

And then I froze. What if I fainted again? What if it happened while I was sitting on the toilet, or walking across the room? What if I collapsed in a heap on the floor and broke something?

Perched on the edge of my hospital bed, and desperate for a pee, I was terrified that I might fall again, and that any broken bones would get in the way of my treatment. Most of all, I was afraid of experiencing that horrible head-buzzing again, and that sense of fading away forever.

Nearly every encounter Violet and I had enjoyed up to this point had been characterized by our silliness and laughter, but Violet was all business when she realized that I was struggling.

She crouched down in front of me and took my hands, as I started to cry. "I'm scared," I whimpered. Violet understood. She immediately instructed me what to do.

"Take deep breaths," she coached.

I did.

"I'm right here," Violet reassured me, and she was. "Now, when you're ready, stand up."

I stood, still taking deep breaths.

And nothing happened to me. No head-buzzing, no room-spinning, and no fear of dying. I paid my visit to the bathroom and came back to bed. I was fine.

Violet, you may have thought I was "cute," but I think you were a lifesaver. Thank you.

Chapter Thirteen: T-Day Minus Two
Food for Thought

I am convinced that there is a factory somewhere that makes the ugliest fabric imaginable, then sells it to the manufacturers of "johnny" coats for hospitals. The johnny coat manufacturers then create shapeless garments that fit no one. They are held together by ribbons that invariably detach in the laundry, leaving the wearer's backside on display for all to see.

I wore johnnies at night, but I made a point of getting dressed in real clothes on all but my worst days. On those days, I didn't care what I looked like. I just wanted to stay in bed.

One day, I sent a selfie to my college friends so they could see what I looked like with no hair. My teal-colored top in the photo received several compliments. My (non) hairdo did, too.

My friend Christine went a step further. She's an artist who frequently consults websites when selecting colors for her paintings. In response to my selfie, Christine sent me the following, which she termed "Color Astrology:"

> *"Teal combines the calming properties of blue with the renewal qualities of green. It is a revitalizing and rejuvenating color that also represents open communication and clarity of thought. For Tibetan monks, teal is symbolic of the infinity of the sea and sky, while it is the color of truth and faith for Egyptians."* Canva.com

> *"People who like the color teal are reliable and independent individuals. They are naturally creative and think for themselves. A teal lover*

has an even temper and a thoughtful disposition. He or she likely has a talent for mediation and finding a compromise."

Interior Designers Institute

Of course, generalizations like these often contain an element of truth. I am reliable, independent, creative, and thoughtful. And, most of the time, I think for myself—unless I'm being treated for cancer, in which case I'm happy to let greater brains than mine do the thinking.

I do not, however, have an even temper—as Michael knows all too well! Nor would I necessarily call myself a good mediator or compromise-finder, because I have a tendency to be swayed by whatever opinion is being   expressed at a given time. Unless the topic is politics...

Still, for the most part, the Interior Designers Institute did a good job of describing this lover of teal, which I most certainly am.

It was Canva's description of the properties of teal, however, that really struck me. Calming, renewing, revitalizing, and rejuvenating; all of these are essential qualities for a person undergoing cancer treatment. Maybe that's what inspired me to pack that particular shirt—a subconscious awareness that it would provide comfort and positive energy.

It was a shame I could only wear my teal shirt once, because one of the rules for transplant patients is that we have to change our clothes every day. With a depleted immune system, we are susceptible to whatever bacteria we might pick up on our garments. When Michael came for his Saturday visits, he would take home a week's worth of clothes, and bring me back the ones he had taken home the previous week. I don't think he'd ever done that much laundry before in his life!

Whether or not they came from the color of my clothes, I periodically needed comfort and positive energy during those long weeks in Boston. I was receiving massive doses of chemo, which takes its toll on a body already weakened by the illness itself.

My broken back was giving me a lot of pain, and, because of my inconvenient pneumonia, I was tethered to an oxygen tank. Add to that my separation from home and loved ones, and my confinement to a room which was basic, to say the least; it's no wonder I felt sorry for myself from time to time!

Along with the regular chemo doses, I was prescribed medication for my back pain. After receiving a new combination of pain medication and muscle relaxant, I sat in my recliner, waiting for it to take effect. Suddenly I heard a conversation taking place behind me, in the adjoining room—except that there was no adjoining room. And no conversation. Then I noticed a dozen or so rabbits that had somehow entered my room, and were hopping around my chair.

Time to press my call button.

The doctor removed that combination of opioid and muscle relaxant from my orders, and I was put back to bed. I'm not sure what they did with the bunnies…

......

When I first arrived at BWH, although I'd been warned that the food left a lot to be desired, I discovered an omelet I really enjoyed: spinach, mushrooms, onions, and Swiss cheese. It was so delicious I ordered it for breakfast every morning.

But, on T-Day-2, I couldn't eat it. Just the sight and smell of it turned my stomach. That total loss of appetite continued through lunch and dinner that, and for the rest of my stay. Not even ramen noodles tempted me.

Considering my aversion to eating, it was surprising that my background noise of choice was the Food Network. Dawn to dusk, I was soothed by the sounds of celebrity chefs Bobby Flay, Ree Drummond, Guy Fieri, their cohorts, and their guests. I marveled at the use of mystery ingredients and unexpected groceries. I rooted for challengers preparing their signature dish.

With so much time on my hands, why did I not read a good book? I don't necessarily mean theology or spiritual enlightenment, although those would have been excellent choices, but a mystery, or a novel... even a magazine? I had brought books with me, and I did open one of them a couple of times, but I simply could not connect with the words on the page. And my freshly charged Kindle sat in a drawer for so long that the battery died.

I couldn't wear teal every day, but watching people cook, seeing raw (often bizarre) ingredients transformed into culinary marvels, somehow calmed and renewed me. On the rare occasion someone beat Bobby Flay, I felt revitalized and rejuvenated.

It's important to know that I was not brought up on culinary expertise. My mother said herself that she was not a good cook. Throughout our childhood, she cycled through a handful of menus: tuna and egg casserole, lamb patties (we called them paddy wags for some reason), meatloaf, baked chicken, and "Risotto alla Lindy"— so-called because an Italian au pair named Lindy taught her how to make it.

Thanksgiving dinner was a gamble, because the turkey was usually bone dry or pink in the middle. One year, however, it was perfect. Our guests looked puzzled when we gave our mother a standing ovation.

One of those guests was Marcel, our "host family" student—a member of a program in which my parents provided hospitality to foreign graduate students. Unfamiliar with Thanksgiving tradition, Marcel had arrived having already eaten. That did not stop him, however, asking for a leg when Dad had finished carving. Then, when seconds were offered, he took the other leg. When the platter went around for the third time, he served himself a portion of breast meat and ended up with the wishbone, which he pulled with Joanie, and lost.

"What did you wish for?" little Joanie asked him.

"I wished turkeys had three legs," he replied.

That perfectly roasted bird was a rare occurrence. Usually we used plenty of gravy to counteract the dry meat, or delayed eating for an hour or more while the bird went back into the oven.

For years I believed I had inherited my mother's shortcomings in the kitchen. But after COVID-19 hit, I discovered recipes. Michael and I each gained around ten pounds during the lockdown, as I prepared salmon Wellington, cheeseburger casserole, steak in pepper sauce, pecan pie, and so much more. It's unfortunate that I didn't think to serve my creations on a tray, thereby rendering them calorie-free!

I will never be the kind of chef who can throw together a tasty dish from whatever is handy. But I have made the life-changing discovery that cooking is therapeutic—more so even than comfort eating.

As my first week at BWH neared its close—I could neither cook nor eat. But thanks to my friends on the Food Network, I did both vicariously.

What I was able to do, and a good thing too, was to brew coffee and tea to drink. And my supply of Diet Coke had the double benefit of tasting good and settling my stomach somewhat.

In addition to those caffeine-laden beverages, on doctors' orders, I drank lots of water. Because I was not permitted to drink tap water, I was going through three to four plastic bottles a day.

One morning, when Diane came on duty, I noticed that she was examining the label on one of my water bottles.

"What are you looking at?" I asked.

"I'm checking to see which states offer cash back for empty bottles," she answered, "because my cousin likes to make a little extra money that way."

Diane was off for a couple of days after that, and I decided to save my empty water bottles for her.

When I had put aside several of them, Florence came in and gathered them up, intending to throw them in the trash.

"Don't throw them away," I said, "I'm saving those for Diane's cousin. She gets money back for recycling them."

Florence didn't say anything more.

The next day, Diane was back, and I proudly showed her the pile of bottles on my window seat. "Those are for you," I announced, "for your cousin!"

"I never said anything about collecting bottles," Diane said. "My cousin? She has plenty to handle."

I could only assume that Florence had reprimanded her for encouraging a patient to hoard trash.

I felt awful.

It was not the first time I had a made what I thought was a kind gesture that backfired. On one occasion, on a crowded subway train, I stood at one end of a carriage near a man with two large, blue suitcases on the floor in front of him. As we reached my stop, he picked up one of the suitcases, and I decided to help him. I grabbed the other suitcase and lifted it down to the platform. When I put it down in front of him, he looked at me quizzically.

"Two is a lot to carry!" I said, breezily.

Just then, another man jumped off the train, with fury on his face. He snatched the suitcase I had apparently stolen from him, and hauled it back onto the train just as the doors were closing.

Neither he, nor the other man, were in the slightest bit interested in my feeble explanation.

Good deeds have unspoken rules. I had broken one of them by not making sure that the first man needed my help—and certainly by not checking that both suitcases belonged to him. They were identical though; I hope the two men ended up with the right ones!

I had broken another rule by not asking Diane if she would like me to save bottles for her, and yet another by telling Florence what I was doing.

And that, like so many incidents in the life of a clergyperson, inspires a mini sermon!

To respond to someone's need, it's important to be sure what that need is. Assumptions can be dangerous. Getting them wrong can do more harm than good.

Equally important is to acknowledge that we can't fix everything. Unless we are positive that we can make a difference, and the other person is agreeable, we should not even try.

Some needs are easy to recognize and fulfill. The need to be heard is almost universal. We all have the ability to listen—although it may come more naturally to some than to others. Another widespread need is for companionship—the simple sharing of physical presence.

Michael's friend Roger, who carpooled to work with him, was an example of that helpful presence. Many years ago, Michael's father died in his sleep while he and Michael's mother and brother were visiting us.

After I called Michael at work with the sad news, Roger drove him home. And then he stayed. All that day, while the rest of us processed our shock and began to grieve, Roger's quiet, solid presence gave us the comfort and reassurance we so badly needed.

In my own pastoral ministry, I have always tried to emulate Roger—to be present without being in the way; to listen without making others feel they have to talk; to provide a source of calm amidst a turmoil of emotions.

I believe that for much of the time I spent at BWH, my willingness to listen encouraged my caregivers to talk—and there was plenty they needed to say as they dealt with staff shortages, demanding patients, and wayward IV stands, not to mention the challenges of their lives outside of work.

During those long weeks, I derived strength from getting myself up and dressed nearly every day— even though I didn't always wear the color teal. And for some peculiar reason, the skills of TV chefs and their creations soothed me.

Perhaps the greatest comfort of all was to recognize that my ministry did not end when I got cancer, or even when I retired. It is a part of me, and always will be, no matter what is going on in my body—and even, perhaps, as I age, my brain!

Along with their practical nursing skills, Florence, Diane, Violet, and the other hospital staff, provided as much pastoral care of me as I did of them.

We looked after each other. That is what our human race needs the most.

Chapter Fourteen: T-Day Minus One
The Big Chill

The day before my transplant, I had one last blast of chemotherapy to endure. Melphalan was different from the two varieties I had been receiving daily, and it was just a single dose.

But what a dose! The infusion lasted just half an hour, but Florence gave me an advance warning:

"I have to tell you, Kate, this chemo can cause painful mouth sores. There's a way to get around it though: you suck on ice for 90 minutes before the infusion. It's called cryotherapy—it constricts the blood vessels in your mouth and makes you less susceptible to side effects."

As always, I did as Florence told me. I was willing to do whatever it took to avoid having sores in my mouth.

But even adding chopped up popsicles, to make it more palatable, didn't make up for the fact that I had a mouthful of ice for an hour and a half. By the time it was all over, I was shivering uncontrollably even under the two warmed blankets Florence provided!

Part of me felt like I would have preferred a mouthful of sores.

As usual, I group-texted my college pals with an update on the life and times of Kate Atkinson, Transplant Patient. And, as usual, Robyn was the first to respond:

"Brrr! Kate stars in The Big Chill. Doing things none of us have ever done!"

When it was all over, Florence made me a lovely cup of tea: strong, hot, with plenty of milk and sugar. Bliss!

And then there was less than a day left before my pristine stem cells would be returned to my bloodstream, to begin their good work of dividing and multiplying, until my entire body was renewed, and lymphoma was nothing but an unpleasant memory.

Florence had some more significant news for me.

"Miss Kate, did you know that tomorrow is a second birthday for you?"

I didn't understand what she meant. "What? Another birthday?"

"Yes, patients call it a birthday, because it's the day you get a new life—from the stem cells. Some transplant patients even have a clergyperson bless the cells. They invite family and friends to witness it. It's an important moment for you."

"New life," I repeated.

A ceremony of life! It sounded wonderful, and Michael and I needed to get a move on to make it happen.

Since it just so happens that I am a member of the clergy, I could bless my own cells. But I would not have anyone physically present, since my family and friends are all over the world, and no one is very near Boston.

But they would be present in a sense. Michael set up a Zoom meeting so that people who are dear to me could be with me (virtually) for the prayer of blessing, and could join in with another prayer Michael would share on the screen. Alternatively, participants could pray their own prayers—or simply offer good wishes and positive energy if they preferred—in their own words and language, as they chose.

And then the baggie would be hung on Bernie, and those healing cells would begin to flow into my veins, while I was surrounded by loved ones wishing me well.

Michael wrote his prayers, while I sent out emails to dozens of friends and family members, inviting them to take part:

Today I finished my last day of pre-transplant chemo, and tomorrow I will receive my "freshly laundered" stem cells. Around here, it's often referred to as a birthday, because it's the day the patient receives new life.

I hope you will be able to join me for this significant moment in my treatment, but of course I understand that it will not be possible for some of you. If that is true of you, perhaps you would join us in spirit, using your own prayers, or whatever light and energy you can send my way.

I was not permitted to send an email to the entire membership of St. Cat's. The Episcopal Church has strict policies around the departure of a priest— whether it is for a job change, a retirement, or something else. For at least a year, there can be no contact between the priest and the church members, which allows the parish to recruit and welcome their new rector, and to form a pastoral relationship with that person, without the interference of the previous incumbent. So, the blanket email was a no-no.

However, because of my unusual circumstances, I was permitted to invite specific parishioners to participate in the Zoom.

The hard part was choosing which parishioners to invite, but I finally narrowed it down to around 30 individuals whom I knew to be deeply spiritual people of prayer. In addition, I invited my siblings, cousins, nephews and nieces, my college gang, several clergy colleagues, and a couple of dozen friends from all corners of my life. I was up until past midnight gathering email addresses, and ensuring that those in different time zones knew when to tune in.

I would be surrounded by people I love, and those who love me, as I celebrated my birth into new life.

Chapter Fifteen: T-Day
Blessings Upon Blessings

The day had finally arrived!

My stem cells were delivered right on schedule, just before noon, by which time my Zoom screen was already full of faces—and the mood was jubilant.

I was high on Benadryl (administered pre-transplant to prevent any undesired reaction), but I tried gamely to introduce everyone to everyone else. The problem was, every time a new participant appeared, the Zoom boxes would shift.

Meanwhile, Cathy (my nurse that day; Florence was off) who had possession of the baggie filled with precious stem cells, was getting more and more agitated about the passing time. We hadn't even started the blessing part!

But I needed the opportunity to look at each one of those beloved faces, and to say a few words about who they were, and what they meant to me: my loyal siblings, Jim, Joanie, and Peter; Peter's wife, Liz; Robyn and three other college pals; fellow members of a spiritual direction group, and of two committees I serve on; parishioners; clergy colleagues; friends and relatives from all over the USA, England, and Belgium, over 60 in all. Dozens more had emailed me to say that they were unable to join us but would be praying for me, or holding me in their heart, at the time of my transplant.

When I had completed the introductions to the best of my ability, Michael prayed his special prayer for me:

"Lord God, I thank you for bringing together this gathering of people who are here to support my beloved wife, who love her too, and have come to pray for her healing or to wish her well, according to the beliefs of each one of us.

And I thank you for those who cannot be present with us, but are sending their prayers or well-wishes from wherever they are.

May Kate know how much she is valued and loved."

Michael followed by leading the gathering in a communal prayer. The cacophony of voices made my heart sing!

"Lord God, you are the creator of all good things.

Nevertheless, we live in a world that has become imperfect and where things can go wrong.

When this happens, we need your healing.

Often you work through people to restore things to the way they are meant to be.

Very often doctors, nurses, and other medical staff are the people you choose to work through to heal those who are sick.

We ask you to take the laundered stem cells and use them to complete the healing of Kate's body so that she can be once again the healthy, vibrant, well person that you made her to be.

Let her know the love that surrounds and supports her as you take her on the journey to wholeness.

Amen."

Next, I offered my own prayers, beginning with prayers of thanksgiving.

I give thanks for the scientists who have devoted years of research to finding cures for so many once fatal diseases, including mine.

I give thanks for the doctors who are overseeing my treatment.

I give thanks for the nurses and care assistants who tend to me daily with such patience, skill, and good humor.

I give thanks for all the support staff without whom none of the medical teams, or their facilities, could function.

Finally, I gave thanks for the people I love—those on my laptop screen, and so many more, near and far, who, in the words of a beautiful song by Martina McBride, were "loving me through it."

I held those cherry-red cells in my hands, and asked God to bless them, and use them to make me well, beginning with some words sent to me by a fellow priest:

"Most Merciful God, Creator and Sustainer of Life, we come before you today, humbled by your great gift of life. In your infinite love, you planted within us these tiny cells that have the power to heal and renew."

I pray, loving God that you would bless these cells today, and in years to come, as they do their good work in my body.

And, as they enter my bloodstream today, may each one of these tiny parts of who I am, reach the places they need to go and bring me to full strength and health.

In Jesus' name. Amen.

Then Cathy hung the baggie on Bernie, and the tube leading to my chest turned that gorgeous red color as new life flowed into my body.

Before the Zoom session finished, all the participants sang Happy Birthday, in a final, wonderful cacophony of love.

That was the first of two stem cell infusions. The second baggie would be delivered at 4:00 that afternoon, and I did request a visit from the chaplain for that one, because I know hospital chaplains don't always get to do the holy work they are called to do.

However, Florence told me there had been one chaplain, from the Mid-West, who almost never got kicked out of the rooms she visited—especially when those rooms were occupied by the male of the species. According to Florence she was young and attractive and had a habit of dressing in short skirts and cowboy boots.

Around twenty minutes after the transplant, in spite of the Benadryl, I had a reaction. I wasn't reacting to the cells, since they were my own; it was the preservative they were suspended in. I started to shiver so violently that my body was jerking all over the bed—much worse than the cryotherapy the day before. Five warmed blankets later, after the preservative had been flushed through me, I started to feel better (and warmer!). And I tolerated the second baggie much better.

When the chaplain arrived for the 4:00 infusion, he stood rather awkwardly by the door as Cathy took my blood pressure. To help him feel more comfortable, I asked him what faith community he belonged to— but apparently that was not an appropriate question, because he suddenly took on a deer-in-the-headlights appearance, looking like he wanted to flee. Clearly that question had been asked of him before, by patients who immediately ejected him if they didn't like his answer.

I hurriedly reassured him that I was just curious because I myself am a priest. But that didn't help matters since he turned out to be a member of a conservative church, and likely didn't approve of women priests! He rattled through his prayer as quickly as possible and bolted.

I felt a little sorry for my second cherry red baggie, getting such a nondescript send-off compared to the noon gathering, so I added a short, silent prayer of my own,

"Thank you, God, for the gift of healing."

My new life had begun.

Chapter Sixteen
Beginnings and Endings

My three siblings and I, as products of an English father and an American mother, are all dual nationals, and we have taken advantage of that status to live, work, and travel freely in the United Kingdom.

I spent my junior year in England's West Country, making several lasting friendships, and also growing closer to my second family, Aunty Betty, Uncle Michael, and cousins, Nick and Philip, with whom I spent many long weekends and holidays.

I returned to the States for my senior year, but, as soon as I had my diploma, I packed up and sailed to Dover on the TSS Stefan Batory ocean liner. England had won my heart, and, despite being thousands of miles away from my nearest and dearest, I would never feel homesick there.

For the next 15 years, I established myself in the direct mail industry, starting in the commercial field and moving on to the non-profit sphere through a combination of circumstances that still amazes me.

I had moved from North London to a little village in Surrey, and was making the daily journey to work by train and subway. I had no car in those days, and I would often walk to the nearest town to do some shopping. A short distance from the grocery store was a building that housed an environmental protection organization I had long supported. Every time I walked past, I would look longingly at that building, especially through a particular window near the entrance, and a desk just inside it.

"I wish I worked there," I would think to myself, every time I walked by. "I wish that were my desk."

Meanwhile, I changed jobs, moving from a North London to a Central London company, which made my commute a little better—but not much. I'd made some good friends at the company I left, and had shared with them my desire to work for the organization near my home. Having only changed employers within the past year, I was not actively job-hunting, but one day I got a phone call from one of those colleagues, telling me about an advertisement she'd seen for the position of Mail Order Manager— at the non-profit I longed to work for!

The deadline for applications was the next day, so I quickly put together my resume and covering letter, and hand-delivered it that evening. I was interviewed a week later, and, within a month, I was offered the position. My desk turned out to be the one I used to gaze at through the window—but now I was on the inside, looking out!

I have shared this remarkable story with many people over the years, some of whom viewed it as evidence of magical wish fulfillment. But I have never thought of it that way. Rather, what I experienced as a desire for that employer, that window, that desk, was God at work in me, preparing me for another, greater life-change that would take place several years down the line.

As I focused on expanding the size of the catalog operation, I hired Fran as my secretary. Fran was not only an excellent employee, she was also a lovely person, and a wonderful addition to our team. When she left, two years later, to have her first child, I stayed in touch with her, and we became close friends.

Despite having been raised by parents who took us to church every week, attending Sunday School and Confirmation classes, singing in the choir, and taking part in youth events, I had strayed considerably during my high school and college years. But I would still attend services at Christmas and Easter, and, as I entered my late twenties, I started to discern an urge for deeper   spiritual connection.

I went to a few services at the church down the road from my house, but that connection failed to happen. It was the same with the church in the next town. Anglicanism is the Established Church in England, so there was no shortage of local congregations in those days, but I simply wasn't finding one where I felt at home.

By this time, Fran had given birth to her second son, Joel, and she invited me to be his godmother. Joel's baptism was taking place at their parish church, during a Sunday evening service, and I was asked to arrive a little early, so we could make sure I knew what I was doing.

As I walked through the door, I was immediately struck by a powerful sense of belonging. The lights were dim, and several candles were burning—giving off a pleasant scent and a comforting glow. Two guitarists played and sang softly while the congregation gathered, and the space was soon filled with quiet conversation and silent prayers. The service itself was welcoming and joyful, led by a young priest with an easy-going manner. I was with friends, celebrating a milestone that I was a part of, and I knew I had found my spiritual home.

That was the church where I became more and more involved in lay ministry. That was the rector who discerned my call to the priesthood even before I did myself. Those were the people who supported me so prayerfully during my time at seminary, and attended my ordination at the cathedral, three years later.

It was the building, the candlelight, and the music that attracted me in the first place, but it was the people who inspired me to keep coming back, and to share my gifts as generously and faithfully as my fellow parishioners shared theirs.

God instilled in me a desire to occupy a certain desk in a certain window. God brought Fran into my life and gave me a godson to cherish. Through Fran, Joel, his brother Tom and sister Philippa, God showed me what it means to be a member of a family of faith.

......

Cancer caused me to miss out on part two of my sabbatical but, the previous Spring, part one had been jam-packed, joyous, and bittersweet.

Michael and I had planned to travel to England and celebrate our silver wedding anniversary at the same hotel where we'd held our evening reception 25 years previously. We made the hotel reservation months in advance. Then it became clear that COVID wasn't going anywhere, so we decided to postpone our trip until sabbatical part two, arriving in time to celebrate my birthday, which I shared with my mother-in-law—who would be turning 95 that September.

Early in the new year, my sister Joanie announced that she would be having Easter dinner with Aunty Betty and our cousins—the first I'd heard that she and her husband, Jeff, were planning a trip to England. I said to Michael, "If Joanie can do it, so can we!" And so we did—but we didn't tell Joanie we were going. Instead, I texted my cousin Nick, told him our plans, and asked him to add Michael and me to the Easter dinner reservation so we could surprise the rest of the family. Then I contacted another cousin, Annette, who lives in Brussels, and suggested that she and her husband also come in on the surprise. She loved the idea and made the arrangements right away with Nick, who was by then full of secrets!

That was our anniversary celebration and Easter surprise arranged, but we had three weeks to fill, and lots of other people to see. We got busy with our plans, booking several different hotels and Airbnbs near family and friends in different parts of England.

Two days before we were due to leave, Michael's brother, David, called to say that their mother was gravely ill with COVID and pneumonia. David and Mother lived in the north of England, and our first planned destination was in the south, but as soon as we got off the plane and collected our car, we drove to Durham and went straight to the hospital.

Mother was unresponsive by that time, but Michael, David, and I sat with her and talked to her, that evening and all the next day. Michael and I had to travel south after that, for obligations that couldn't be altered, but we were glad we'd had the chance to say goodbye to dear Mother. She died two days later.

On Easter Day, Michael and I arrived early at the pub where the family gathering would take place. We told the serving staff about the surprise we had planned, then sat down at a table for two behind a large potted plant. Joanie and Jeff arrived and were taking their seats at the big table Nick had reserved, when we emerged from our hiding place and shouted "Surprise!"—much to the amusement of the servers.

Our Dad had loved surprising his loved ones, and all four of his offspring inherited that trait. Joanie was beside herself—for the second time, because she and Jeff had run into our Belgian cousins the previous evening. Not only had they all come down for dinner at the same time, but their rooms were across the hall from each other!

The only flaw in an otherwise joyful celebration, was that our younger cousin, Philip, was unable to join us due to a problem he was having with his leg. We spent time with him after the meal, and it was clear that he was in considerable pain from an as yet undiagnosed condition.

Not long after we returned to the States, we got the news. Philip had an aggressive form of bone cancer which had already spread to his lungs and other parts of his body. He died less than two months later, aged 59, the beloved baby of the cousins. We were heartbroken.

But during our time in England, we were blissfully unaware of the sorrow we had in store. One of our Airbnb sojourns was in a little guest cottage in the grounds of a magnificent country house. It even had its own Royal Mail box!

The guest house kitchen was, surprisingly, not very well equipped, but I managed to cobble together a fancy risotto, using a recipe from a British food magazine. We had invited my longstanding friend, Fran to lunch, along with another dear friend of over 30 years' standing, Janet, whom I had met through Fran. We had a lovely time—simply picking up where we had left off, as good friends do. Fran enjoyed her meal, but she mentioned that she had recently had a bout of gastric flu and was happy to be feeling better so she could enjoy my risotto.

Two months later, the day after Philip died, I had an email from Fran, saying she had liver cancer that had metastasized to all her organs. She died less than a week later—only 60 years old. Her two sons, my godson Joel, and his brother Tom, took part in the blessing of my stem cells. Those dear young men supported me in my cancer treatment despite the fact that their cherished mother had not survived hers.

We were still in England for Mother's funeral, which took place the week after our anniversary. It was a lovely service, with touching eulogies from Michael and David, and many friends filling the pews at the church where the family were longstanding members—and where   Michael and I had met. Then, over the next two days, we engaged in what David termed "excursion therapy:" day trips to beautiful places in the Yorkshire Dales and the Lake   District. It was just what we all needed—and a wonderful tribute to Mother, for whom family was all-important.

If we had stuck to our temporarily revised plan to go to England in September, we would not have had the chance to be with Mother, Philip, and Fran, for the last time. We would not even have been able to travel, because September was when my cancer journey began.

It's true: God does move in mysterious ways.

Chapter Seventeen: T-Day Plus One
Blood Counts and Trolls

Yesterday's stem cell event had sparked a flurry of texts from my college gang:

"What a beautiful party! Happy new birthday. You are such an inspiration, Kate. May those laundered stem cells multiply quickly to restore you to strength and health. Much love."

"Agree!! We love you so!!!!"

"It was such an honor to be with and pray with all of you. Many blessings, Kate. You are indeed loved and cherished by so many!"

"Amazing to know it is done! You did it!!! What an incredible day—one you've been waiting for so long."

"So happy that you were surrounded by such a great big bunch of people who love you. That was a Zoom like no other before!!! XXOO"

I received emails too, both from people who had participated in the Zoom gathering, and from some who hadn't been able to be there, but let me know they had been with us in spirit. It meant the world to me to know that so many people, from so many corners of my life, had accompanied me on that momentous occasion. And they weren't going anywhere; I was never alone.

Now it was time to focus on regaining my strength.

The chemo had started doing what it was supposed to do. My blood was still being stripped of platelets, red and white cells, and every type of immunity that had ever been achieved through vaccination—including all my   infant and childhood shots. I was effectively a newborn baby in an adult body, and I would have a lot of catching up to do.

But first we had to let the progression continue until my blood counts reached their lowest point then started to build back up again. This is why I had to remain in the hospital for another two weeks following the transplant.

Every morning, at around 4:30, my blood was drawn and sent to the lab. The results were then recorded both on my computer record, and also on a poster stuck to the wall in my room. The poster would be presented to me on my departure—presumably to be framed and put on display in my living room.

Florence hated filling in the numbers on the poster, but another nurse, Missy, loved doing it. Missy also loved tidying the cubby filled with IV supplies, especially after Florence had been on duty and had thrust in handfuls of saline syringes and alcohol wipes, willy nilly.

Missy made me promise not to tell Florence that she was the one who had tidied the cubby, but I think Florence probably guessed. I wonder if Missy ever got the Starfish award...

I have always yearned to be a tidy, well-organized person, but it has never quite happened. Growing up, we moved a lot, living in a succession of rented houses vacated by college professors on sabbatical for a year or two. When we finally bought a house of our own, our parents chose private education for their four children, over interior decoration, which I found incredibly frustrating, ingrate that I was.

My solution to the lack of domestic elegance was to save my babysitting money—which took a long time since our parents only allowed us to charge 50 cents an hour—and use it to decorate my bedroom. I purchased carpet and wallpaper, which my father taught me to hang. I also selected an inexpensive set of matching curtains and bedspread.

My parents contributed a suite of furniture which came from a 1970s iteration of Craigslist.

Looking back, my bedroom transformation resembled nothing more—or less—than a room in a cheap motel. But I loved it.

I did not, however, keep my fancy room tidy. I always had some sort of craft project going, so there were materials all over the floor, intermingled with the clothes I didn't bother to put away. This trend continued through my college years, so that, whenever I returned for a weekend or vacation, my mother would take one look at the mess and remark, "I see Kate's home!"

But one place was always in impeccable order; that was Trollsville.

From the ages of six and eight, my younger brother, Peter, and I collected trolls. We had regular trolls, large-sized trolls, pencil topper trolls, gum machine trolls, even horse, cow, lion, and giraffe trolls. They all had names and personalities, and they all talked in an accent that sounded somewhat Germanic.

And they were hilarious.

Peter and I would take our favorites (Alfred, Muzzer Nature, Hubby, and Supertroll) with us on family road trips, and our parents would be in stitches in the front seat of the car, listening to the squeaky dialogues in   progress behind them.

Occasionally our mother or father would attempt to interject an addition to the trolls' conversation. Their attempts were invariably met with the query, "Who sed zat?"

Trollsville was home base: a four- by eight-foot sheet of plywood, marked out in roads and lawns, with houses made from building blocks glued down. There was a school (for the little pencil-topper children), a church (where Rev. Casper led services, dressed in his clerical collar), a zoo, a farm, a papier mâché cave for the cave trolls, and a raised corner where the hillbilly family lived. For around five years, Peter and I would "play trolls" every chance we got; it was our favorite pastime, and no one else knew how.

One Spring vacation, when our brother Jim was growing proficient in film production (his eventual career), we made a stop-action movie using his Super-8 camera, painstakingly moving the trolls millimeters at a time—with the final effect, once the film had returned from the developer (this was 1969, after all), of trolls gliding around their village while Supertroll saved the day.

Film-making was just one of many creative outlets for my siblings and me. Our passion for the performing arts had been passed down to us by our mother, who was involved in amateur dramatics for most of her life. She took a break to raise her four rambunctious children, then she was back to treading the boards. Madame Arcati in Blithe Spirit, the Sonia part in Godspell (singing Turn Back, O Man), Miss Hannigan in Annie... she played dozens of "mature" roles, and was much loved by the undergrads she often acted with.

Taking after my mother as a character actor, I was usually cast as a crone, a prostitute, or a posh elderly lady. But that was while I was still at school and college; my acting career tailed off considerably once I entered the world of work.

An aspect of ministry could be compared to stage acting, however. That is not to say that one's faith or spirituality is an act, but there are certainly times when a member of the clergy needs to project one mood, when, inside, they feel completely different.

I was heartbroken when my mother died. And it was compounded when I made the cross-country trip afterwards, to pack up her things and move my father into a smaller assisted living unit. Because of his Alzheimers, he was not aware that he had lost the love of his life—the dear woman he had always referred to as "my better half." Just four months later, he too passed away—although we had already lost him years earlier, once that cruel disease took hold.

Grief is a heavy, stifling burden for anyone to carry. When one is responsible for helping others carry their own burdens, one's personal grief can grow even heavier and more suffocating.

I remember talking to a parishioner at coffee hour, shortly after I returned from getting my father organized, less than two weeks after my mother's death. He said some words of sympathy, and, before I could even thank him, he launched into an account of how he had felt when his mother died. I had to be the pastor, not the pastored; that was my job.

Michael could see that I was grieving deeply, but suppressing my pain, and he was worried about me. So he invited Robyn to come for the day, one Sunday, without telling me. (My family's love of surprises has rubbed off on him!) I was presiding at the 10:00 worship service that morning, when I spotted a familiar face in one of the side pews. Robyn! I couldn't believe it!

At lunch afterwards, Robyn commented on how happy I had seemed, leading worship and preaching. I can't say that it was an act, because I genuinely do find joy in doing those things, but I was hiding a grief that was eating me up inside, and which I refused to reveal to the people in my care.

Thankfully I had my loving husband and close friends with whom I could share my true feelings, and the pain diminished over time, but I had found it necessary to put on an act—to be the strong, non-anxious, and pastoral presence my congregation expected, and needed me to be. I imagine there's not a single ordained minister who doesn't recognize what I am describing.

During my two battles with cancer, there have certainly been times when I acted as though I felt better than I did, but that was never the case at BWH. That's because my nursing team knew exactly what I was going through, whether I told them or not. They anticipated every symptom and they answered every one of my questions, patiently and knowledgeably.

We all have to be good actors from time to time, but it's important to have people with whom we can be our real selves.

Chapter Eighteen: T-Day Plus Two
A Johnny Coat Day

I woke up on this second day post-transplant, feeling dreadful. When the team of doctors visited later that morning, they explained why: my blood counts were dropping dramatically, as anticipated, and I was being drained of my physical life force. Thank God, my spiritual life force was going strong. I'm convinced God used my cellphone to assure me of that.

A little ping informed me that a communication had arrived. It was a Google memory from a year ago, a short video of Ernie racing into our bedroom and leaping onto the bed for his daily, morning cuddles. The sight of that adorable pup, and the reminder of what I was missing, made me cry. And cry. And cry. As tears poured down my cheeks, I realized I was weeping for so much more than my far-away puppy.

I was missing people too, especially those who lived furthest away. And those who were no longer with us.

Every time Michael and I made a trip to England, I would meet up with another dear friend from my days at the non-profit. Margaret and I were the same age and had much in common—from our family make-up, to our taste in music and film, to the things that made us laugh. For years we would meet early every weekday morning and visit the gym together for a pre-work work-out.

After Michael, Alex, and I moved to the States, each time we returned to England, Margaret and I would spend a day together, relaxing at a spa. On one of those occasions, we tried hard not to stare at the actor, Emma Thompson, who was seated at the next lunch table!

Shortly before we made our trip during sabbatical part one, I emailed Margaret to say we were coming, and to ask which spa she would like to visit. It had been a while since we had been in touch, so, when I didn't hear back, I assumed she had changed her email address and wrote to her by snail mail instead. There was still no response.

We had only been in England for a few days when I ran into another one-time work colleague, Mabel.

"I've been trying to get in touch with Margaret, but she isn't responding. Do you know if she's moved?"

"Margaret?" Mabel replied, looking shocked. "She died just before Christmas."

Unbeknownst to me, my dear friend had been gone for four months. Cancer had claimed another victim, far too young.

So, as the sight of my sweet puppy triggered copious tears, I wept for Margaret, and Philip, and Fran, and Michael's mother. I wept for my own mother, and my dear father who was robbed of a full life years before he died. I wept for the ministry I loved and had been forced to relinquish. I wept for everything and everyone I had ever lost—and, frankly, I wept because I felt sorry for myself.

As soon as I realized that at least some of my tears were self-indulgent, I stopped crying. Yes, lives cut short were deserving of grief, but I had been blessed to have those people in my life for as long as I had. Not only that, but they had each contributed, in different ways, to the wondrous direction my life had taken.

Two days previously, I had been given my life back again; living abundantly would be as much a tribute to those loved ones as it would be fulfilling for me. I could cry for the life my loved ones had lost, but I didn't need to cry for myself.

So what that my room was spartan, and all I could see out the window were brick walls and more windows? So what that I'd lost my appetite? Or my freedom? Or my hair? Those inconveniences were temporary— and they were a small price to pay for the gift of life. God had reminded me of that through Ernie's appearance on my phone, and my tearful reaction.

I washed my face and laughed at myself in the mirror.

However, recognizing my foolishness did not make me feel any better physically. I was so weak that I could barely make it to the bathroom, and, because I was beginning to experience another unpleasant side effect, intestinal in nature, I needed to visit the bathroom frequently. Florence's solution was to place the commode next to the bed. At my request, she even dug up an air freshening block for my windowsill.

Speaking of odors, when Diane came in that morning, she commented that I no longer smelled of the preservative from my stem cells. I had absolutely no awareness of this, but that aroma was very strong, and had been seeping through my pores—in much the same way garlic does. Apparently the whole room reeked of it—in spite of the air freshener. Thanks for telling me, Diane!

Body odor aside, I felt lousy. This was one of those days when I stayed in my ugly johnny coat and did not leave my bed unless I had to. The Food Network kept me company, and I slept on and off until mid-afternoon, when I finally felt strong enough to sit up and drink a cup of tea.

......

The rector with whom I served my curacy, from 1996 to 2000, had no tolerance for illness—his own or anyone else's. This was unfortunate because I was afflicted by a number of health issues during those four years, including two surgeries, two miscarriages, and a mystery illness that landed me in the hospital for over a week.

Rev. George had spent several years in Rwanda, working on a Bible translation, and he and his young family were there at the start of the genocide. Having witnessed the worst extremes of human suffering, he viewed ailments like mine as minor, and any time taken away from church work as malingering. As a result, I did my best to push through whatever health challenge I was facing, and to carry out my responsibilities even when I needed time to rest and recover. The most difficult thing I had to do was to give a sermon while I was miscarrying. I was on the preaching schedule, so I fulfilled my duty, even while our future child was leaving my body.

Rev. George was an interesting person in many ways—a combination of intolerances like the one I've described, and a creative and humorous take on life. He was homophobic and even rather misogynistic, but, in spite of my feelings about his views, he made me laugh.

Our diocese offered a monthly clergy day—which was sometimes edification and sometimes pure entertainment. On one occasion, the activity was a trip to a nearby winery, where there was a tour of the premises in a small train with three carriages. One of the spaces we traveled through had a sign that read "Alarmed Area." I happened to glance at the carriage behind mine, and there was Rev. George, hands in the air, mouth open, pretending to be alarmed. He was impossible, and I couldn't help liking him.

At BWH, on the transplant ward, no one judged me for feeling lousy, but I suppose a little bit of George had rubbed off on me all those years ago. Eventually, I forced myself to get up and sit in my recliner—but I didn't change out of my johnny.

Chapter Nineteen: T-Day Plus Three
Lyrics, Loss, and Love

This morning Robyn introduced a guessing game to our group text.

"Good morning, all. This is your Saturday morning Mystery Song Lyric. Can you guess what song this line is from? Hint: You all know the song, and it's from the 70s."

She then quoted a line that I guessed was from Carole King's Tapestry. That happens to be one of my favorites, so I won!

We were treated to one more mystery line before settling down to the rest of our early morning chat, from the iconic song about walking boots. All four players were quick to respond:

"Yup, got that one."

"Nancy Sinatra's one-hit wonder."

"Yeah. Whatever happened to her?"

"She got old and hung up her boots."

Today was a red-letter day because my hubby came to visit. We had agreed before I was admitted to BWH that he would only visit me on Saturdays, because we wanted to save up his time off and use it when I was back home again. Today was the day, and I felt stronger than ever just anticipating Michael's visit. Unlike the day before, when I stayed in bed like a lump, I took a shower, brushed my teeth, polished my bald head, and got dressed.

Michael and I had met nearly 30 years before, when I was at seminary in the North of England, and started worshiping at a local church where he was a member. He tells me that he had noticed me the moment I walked in for the first time.

I didn't notice him, however, because I was dating Jerry, someone I had met at my church in Surrey.

The summer of my first year at seminary, Jerry and I flew to California to visit Joanie, who had recently had her first baby, Katie. One morning, Jerry fed Katie two bottles in a row (she usually had only one), and she vomited all over his cellphone. His angry reaction set off alarm bells in my mind, and I was on high alert for the rest of our stay.

I once read an article, written by a psychologist, that described what he termed the "X-factor." This factor, he observed, is what fuels a romantic relationship. It's that indefinable feeling that occurs when one is in the presence of the other, or even spots the other person across a room.

At Heathrow Airport, on our return from California, I caught sight of Jerry returning from the men's room, and felt nothing. I realized then that whatever X had once factored into our relationship, it was gone. I broke up with him within the week.

Three months after that trip, tragedy struck our family, when, just before Christmas, little Katie succumbed to Sudden Infant Death Syndrome, commonly known as S.I.D.S. She was four months old, the light of her parents' life. Our shared grief was excruciating.

My family was not new to grief. Muth had lost her father, our adored Pa, when he was only 63, and Dad's father was just 72 when he died. By this time, both my grandmothers were gone as well, and both of Muth's brothers had died by suicide, caused by bi-polar disease and the ravages of WWII.

We had all—especially our parents—weathered those losses and moved on, but this loss was different. Katie was an infant, with her whole life ahead of her.

That little baby was full of light, and had an uncanny gift of enhancing the mood in whatever place Joanie and her first husband, Cam, took her. Joanie's volunteer work often brought her into nursing homes, where Katie would gurgle and laugh, and delight even the gruffest or most vacant elder. Her grandparents, aunts, uncles, and cousins, doted on her almost as much as her proud   parents did.

When that beautiful light went out, and all our hopes and dreams for Katie's future trickled away, the pain was agonizing.

The priest who took Katie's memorial service had a deep understanding of how bereft we were over the earthly life Katie would never experience. He expressed it exquisitely:

"We thought we would be celebrating Katie's first Christmas with her, but instead she is celebrating Jesus' birthday with him. We thought we would teach Katie to walk, but instead God is teaching her to soar. We thought we would teach Katie to talk, but instead God is teaching her to sing. We thought we would be able to hold onto Katie for longer, but instead she is being held in God's arms forever."

One of my favorite photographs of Katie shows her smiling in my arms, with Joanie's arms wrapped around us both. And there is another pair of arms wrapped around all three of us. They may not be visible in the photograph, but they are gloriously visible in heaven. God will love and care for Katie, always. No harm will ever come to her.

The dreadful pain we experienced from the moment we first heard the news of Katie's death, was lessened somewhat when we were able to grieve together. We were able to laugh together, too, especially when we watched a video created by a friend of Joanie and Cam, with all their favorite clips of Katie. It included her first taste of cereal—just two days before she died—and a wonderful sequence of her rolling over from back to front, which had the entire audience straining on her behalf!

Katie's ashes, a tiny handful, light as a breath, were buried in the Garden of Remembrance at Joanie's church. And every August, the month Katie was born, the bush planted over her spot is a mass of pink roses.

It is unfortunate that my one and only visit with my tiny niece was tainted by the behavior of my ex, but he was well and truly out of the picture when I returned to England after Katie's memorial service in California.

Life became somewhat quiet then, as I struggled through my grieving process and tried to stay on top of such challenges as New Testament Greek and systematic theology.

That year I was officially on placement at St. Jude's, the church I had begun to attend when I first arrived at seminary. The Children's Act had recently been published, and compliance was required from any organization involved in activities for children and youth. Including churches. There was an active middle school youth group at St. Jude's at that time, which was being led by a rather shy young man named Michael Atkinson.

In order to comply with the Children's Act, and to make sure there was no hanky-panky between the youngsters, the youth group had to have two leaders—one male and one female. And, as part of my seminary placement, I was asked to be the co-leader, working in partnership with Michael. It's funny that the Children's Act was concerned about hanky-panky between the youth, but not between the leaders...

Little did I know that my seminary placement would change my life!

There was a meeting of all Sunday School teachers shortly after I returned from Katie's service in California. I was still in that numb stage of grief, where everything seemed to be happening through a layer of cotton, but I was aware of profound, genuine kindness when Michael expressed his condolences.

As Michael and I continued with our Sunday morning ministry for the rest of that year, I gradually emerged from the cocoon of my sorrow. Then, as we approached a holiday weekend near the end of summer term, some fellow students asked me to look after their two children while they took a short break together. I was happy to agree, and prepared to move into their house for three days.

I had recently seen a poster about a multi-faith picnic, which was scheduled to take place in the grounds of the local Roman Catholic seminary that coming Saturday. Thinking it would be a good event to take my two charges to, and not having the necessary vehicle in which to get to it, I asked Michael if he would like to join us and take us in his car. He accepted readily, and instantly invited me to his house, for dinner and a movie, that Wednesday.

The evening arrived, and Michael prepared chicken, rice, salad, and strawberries with cream. Not only was the meal delicious, but Michael insisted on doing the dishes as soon as we had finished eating. "I can never leave the washing up," he confessed. I was dumbstruck.

The movie Michael had chosen was *Patriot Games*, which we watched from two separate armchairs. When it was over, he drove me back to my dorm, and that was it, the end of a lovely, uneventful evening. I found myself looking forward to Saturday's picnic, and, three days later, there it was—along with unrelenting rain.

But church folks are nothing if not resourceful. We spread our blankets on the floor of one of the seminary's common rooms, and enjoyed the picnic lunches we had packed. Michael was great with the kids. And Michael was great with me. I was beginning to fall—and I believe the same was true of him.

The next afternoon, my friends came back from their get-away, and invited Michael and me to dinner. At the end of the evening, as we were preparing to leave, I remembered some smoked fish I had left in their freezer. When I went into the kitchen to retrieve it, Michael followed.

Suddenly he took hold of me for the kind of kiss that should feature in a romantic comedy! I say romantic because it was; I say comedy because it took place in a kitchen. "Someone's in the kitchen with Dinah... strumming on the old banjo..."

And that was it. At the age of 39, I had found my husband, and Michael, at the age of 38, had found his wife. Geriatric though we were, we knew a soulmate when we saw one. The X factor had arrived in no uncertain terms!

We have been married for over 25 years, and we still haven't hung up our boots.

Chapter Twenty: T-Day Plus Four
Ordained

Michael had arrived in my hospital room around noon the previous day, and I took a picture of him coming through the door, weighed down with bags of items I had asked him to bring, wearing the obligatory mask and latex gloves, and grinning so hard, it showed in his eyes.

Michael hadn't had lunch yet, and I hadn't either, so I ordered enough food for us both: soup for me, Caesar salad with chicken, an egg salad sandwich, chips, and a cookie for Michael. The hospital keeps track of how much patients eat; they must have thought my appetite had miraculously returned!

When we had finished eating, we turned to the most important order of the day: Yahtzee. Scrabble and Yahtzee are our two favorite games, and I had brought travel versions of both.

I found out later that our activity had caused some consternation in the nurses' station, where no one could identify the sound of the dice rattling in their plastic cup! Michael got two Yahtzees and trounced me, and then it was time for dinner—and another overflowing tray of food to share.

Our favorite games weren't restricted to dice and letter tiles; there were two TV game shows we favored as well. My parents had discovered *Wheel of Fortune* and *Jeopardy* many years back and had become devoted fans. Every weeknight, from 7:00 to 8:00, they would be glued to the television, shouting out the answers. Actually, Muth did most of the shouting; she was one smart cookie!

Several years later, I noticed *Wheel of Fortune* and *Jeopardy* listed in the channel guide, and suggested to Michael that we watch them that evening in honor of Muth and Dad. We did—and we were hooked.

Judging by the commercials that accompany these shows, the target audience is of an age that needs funeral insurance, panic buttons, and incontinence products. So far, we haven't needed any of the above products, but we know how to find them should that change.

Michael's visit ended with the two of us glued to the television, shouting out answers. I hope we didn't cause more consternation in the nurses' station...

Then it was time for my hubby to hit the road. We wouldn't see each other for another week, and we weren't even allowed to hug. But at least he'd finally be able to take off his latex gloves. It was a sign of how much he loves me that he wore them, as instructed, throughout his visit—sweaty hands and all.

Michael and I often comment that we wish we had met earlier—when we were in our twenties perhaps. But then Michael says that I probably wouldn't have liked him because he was such a nerd, and I tell him that he probably wouldn't have liked me because I was a smoker, not quitting until I was thirty.

But it was unfortunate that it took us so long to see the light in my final year at seminary, because I was only going to be in Durham for two more weeks after our *Patriot Games* date. After graduation, I would be heading south to be ordained and begin my curacy in Surrey. We did our best to make up for lost time during those two short weeks, but I still had papers to hand in, and Michael, most inconsiderately, had a job to go to.

Michael lived within walking distance of the seminary, and would visit most evenings, crossing a bridge down the road from my dorm. When it was time for him to head home again, I would walk with him as far as the middle of the bridge, where we would say goodnight, often taking as long as fifteen minutes to do so. We must have made the ducks blush.

......

Michael had made plans, months earlier, for a vacation in Spain with his brother, David, which meant that he was unable to be present for my ordination to the diaconate. Yet many other loved ones were there. My parents had flown over from America; my cousins had come from Belgium; and dozens of friends and relatives traveled from all over England, including huge contingents from St. James, my sponsoring parish, and St. Simeon's, the parish I would be serving as curate.

Thirteen other ordinands were present with me for the ceremony at Guildford cathedral that day. We were ushered into a common room before the service—a mixture of young and not-so-young, male and female, conservative and progressive, united by our desire to serve God and to make a difference in a world that was losing its way.

But first, I had some peppermints to hand out. The combination of excitement and nerves had caused a few dry mouths, so everyone took a mint gratefully, and we popped them into our mouths.

At that very moment, the Dean of the Cathedral came into the room to pray for us. He offered his prayer, we all said "Amen," and then there was a communal crunch as each of us made sure we wouldn't be ordained while sucking on a peppermint.

The service was an unforgettable combination of solemnity and celebration, as we made the vows that would shape our words and actions for the rest of our lives, and as our voices joined in hymns that resounded throughout that glorious space. Guildford Cathedral was less than 100 years old, a soaring structure of pale bricks (topped by an angel weathervane!) that had been the cause of much controversy in its day, due to its modern design. It was also featured in the movie *The Omen*, in the scene where Damien has a meltdown when his parents try to take him to a church wedding.

Back in the 1940s, when funds were being raised to build Guildford Cathedral, one could "buy" a brick. My parents, who hadn't met each other yet, each sponsored a brick, and our family legend is that their two bricks ended up side by side.

After the service, my entourage headed to the home of Alicia and Bill, a couple from St. James who had become good friends of mine. They'd had a large tent erected in their backyard, and, in partnership with my parents, were hosting a party in my honor.

Another friend, whose business was videography, filmed the event—including a hilarious moment where Muth can be seen pressing a wad of cash into Alicia's hand, paying her share.

I was asked to say a few words, which included my gratitude for my parents: Dad, "who taught us never to be afraid to try something new," and Muth, "whose solution, whatever challenge might be occurring in our life, was 'Go to church.'"

The only person missing from that wonderful day was my Michael. Later, when we were back home, and everyone had gone except my parents and a few other close relatives, the phone rang. My family said they could tell instantly who was at the other end of the line, by the loving tone of my voice.

I hope I still sound like that when I'm talking to Michael. I know I did when he spent the afternoon with me, playing Yahtzee and eating my food. I done good.

Earlier that day, after visiting the bathroom, I had noticed that the hem of my pants was wet. The shower was right next to the toilet, and had no pan to contain the water, so I figured the floor hadn't been mopped properly. I mentioned it to Missy, and—not surprisingly, with Missy on duty—it was taken care of immediately.

But then it happened again, the next time I used the bathroom. This time further investigation revealed a leak in the base of the toilet, and a maintenance man was called.

He arrived promptly, took a look, and informed us that there was a leak in the base of the toilet. Duh. He also told us that a plumber would have to be brought in, and that I would have to vacate my room while the repair work was being done.

When a person (me) is being kept in near sterile conditions, vacating a room does not mean sitting in the hallway with a book for an hour or two. It means being moved to another air tight room and, since all the rooms on our floor were occupied, it meant moving to a different floor. We were informed by maintenance that they had called an emergency plumber, who would probably arrive within the hour. It was already nearly 9:00 at night, and I was still in my original room, with a towel wrapped around the base of the toilet.

Finally, at 11:00, it was clear that there would be no plumber materializing before morning, and I was allowed to go to sleep.

The next morning, I had barely gotten dressed when a wheelchair arrived to whisk me away. The plumber was in the building and, since it was Sunday, the sooner he could get started, the better (and cheaper). I grabbed my laptop and off we went.

This was the day for our college gang to have its regular, bi-weekly Zoom meeting. The timing could not have been better. I was in a strange room, with nurses I didn't know, and I was not feeling very well. But, at 12:30, I could open my laptop and gaze on a screenful of dear faces. I could also receive lots of compliments on my (non-)hairdo!

There was a good deal of news to share. Sue was preparing her late mother's house to sell; Robyn was doing lots of heavy gardening (which she loves), while her 300-year-old house was being re-sided and painted; Lorrie was going to see a play at her local theatre; and Ashley was getting ready to travel to Africa for a photography workshop. My news? I was sitting in a barren room, with unfamiliar nurses, while my toilet was being fixed.

But friends of decades' standing were there to help. Something very special exists with good friends— especially those from the days of misspent youth. Not that we were hooligans, but some of us (especially Robyn and me) got up to plenty of mischief when we should have been writing papers or studying for exams.

I have always maintained that our college years are mainly about learning to learn—academics, of course, but also life skills. I can't say that I put the best of those life skills into practice the moment I graduated, but they definitely came into play as I got older. And now I'm a priest! Who knew?

In the middle of the afternoon, the wheelchair arrived to take me back to my floor, my room, and my familiar nurses.

It nearly didn't happen. Florence told me later that the on-duty Hospital Administrator had wanted to leave me on the fourth floor for the rest of my stay, but the sixth floor staff had argued it would be simpler to bring me back again.

It's good to have friends.

Chapter Twenty-one: T-Day Plus Five
Otherwise Engaged

This morning's blood draw showed that my counts were nearing their nadir (meaning lowest point, via Middle English and Middle French, and from the Arabic nadhīr, meaning opposite—according to the Merriam-Webster Dictionary). Nadir is not a word in common usage, in my experience, and, sure enough, nearly every time I used it in conversation with a non-medical person, I had to provide a definition. I still used it though, because it sounds so much fancier than "my counts are nearing their lowest point."

Michael does know what nadir means, because his college degree was in linguistics. His brain is one of the things I love about him, and his vocabulary is a veritable aphrodisiac.

Even though it was a mutual decision to limit Michael's visits to once a week, there were times when I missed him so much that it was all I could do to stop myself from picking up the phone and begging him to jump in the car.

I never did succumb to that longing, but I did find that I spent many hours thinking about my cherished husband, and revisiting memories of some of our special times together.

For my 40th birthday, Michael took me to Paris. We traveled on the Eurostar train, through the Channel Tunnel, and had three nights in a small hotel with a large breakfast buffet.

We visited the Mona Lisa at the Louvre; we marveled at Notre Dame, pre-fire; we cruised the Seine; we hiked up the many steps to Montmartre; and we canoodled in several scenic locations. But we did not get engaged—much to the surprise of our acquaintances, who fully expected me to come back wearing a ring. After all, Paris is the city of romance, and we were not getting any younger. But Michael didn't want to be predictable, and proposing in Paris is nothing if not predictable!

A month later, Michael was visiting again, and was standing beside me at the kitchen sink, washing the dishes. All of a sudden, he turned to me, with dripping hands, and said, "Will you marry me?" I burst out laughing. But he meant it, and we went out that very afternoon to buy a ring.

I was a fiancée!

Just a week before our engagement, Joanie had given birth to her second daughter, Carly, and now we had two reasons to travel to America—to meet my new niece and to show off my betrothed. We arrived in San Francisco the day before Thanksgiving, and Joanie and baby Carly were at the airport to collect us. Muth and Dad had traveled down from Oregon, to meet their new granddaughter and future son-in-law, so it was a jolly gathering—and Michael felt well and truly welcomed into the family.

It was too much to expect Joanie to prepare a Thanksgiving dinner for six, less than a month after giving birth, so we all went out to a huge family restaurant where a special holiday meal was being served. I am convinced that it was that meal that made Michael decide he wanted to live in the United States: our oval plates were the size of serving platters, and were piled high. Every serving was enough for a family of four—and even Michael couldn't finish his meal.

Carly, who had instantly captured our hearts, slept in her carrier throughout the meal—blissfully unaware that she was helping to mend those hearts. We will never forget her sister, Katie, but Carly brought us her own brand of healing and joy.

Michael and I agreed on a wedding date at the end of April, because Michael's birthday is in early April, and it would mean only one year between our ages on the marriage license. After all, I wouldn't want the City Registrar to think I was a cougar!

Lying on my hospital bed, drained of energy, I remembered with awe the three days leading up to our wedding day, when I managed a flurry of errands, dress fittings, and airport runs on top of my usual church duties. Family members were flying in from Boston, New York, and Brussels, the groom would be driving down from Durham with his brother, David, followed the next day by their parents. My little church house was soon bursting at the seams!

Elaine, the parishioner who made the dresses for me, Joanie, and our eight-year-old niece, Annie, had been a seamstress for Harrods, in London, before she retired. Her work was so exquisite that one could wear her garments inside-out and the seams wouldn't show. Her trademark when making a wedding dress, was to sew a tiny blue bow inside the waist—so the bride would always be wearing "something blue." I called my dress a "Parish Original."

Annie looked lovely in her flower girl dress, white with blue flowers. While Elaine was turning her around so she could pin up her hem, Annie couldn't take her eyes off herself in the mirror—swiveling her head until it was practically on backwards.

As Matron of Honor, Joanie had the pleasant duty of organizing my hen night, Brit-speak for bachelorette party. Cookery was its theme. Joanie had sent each guest a blank recipe card with their invitation, on which they were asked to write a favorite recipe. The cards were then presented to me, each with an item that went with the recipe. For example, a spaghetti sauce recipe came with a pasta server, and a cheesecake recipe came with a springform pan.

Dinner was Joanie's "Pre-Nuptial Penne" followed by chocolate cake, and there was much hilarity—especially when I unwrapped a meat-tenderizing mallet with a recipe card noting that the mallet could also be used on one's husband should the need arise.

While the hens were cackling, the roosters were at the pub, enjoying a meal and a glass or two of warm beer. Dad returned before the others, to Muth's displeasure—because she wanted to stay for more fun with the hens. But eventually everyone went home (or wherever their beds were), and we were another day closer to the big event.

There are plenty of nadirs in these lives of ours, but many more apexes. The week of my wedding was full of them. Remembering that time, and marveling over the joy Michael had brought into my life that day at the kitchen sink, I could almost ignore my present loneliness and weakened condition.

How I missed my hubby!

Chapter Twenty-two: T-Day Plus Six
Wedding Bells

Today I found out what happens when a transplant patient's platelets reach their nadir: they get a platelet transfusion! And this morning's blood work results indicated that I needed that transfusion. Soon a new baggie was attached to my dingle-dangles and bright yellow sludge slowly started its journey into my veins.

Peggy, a young clergy colleague, whose body produces a surplus of platelets, donates them regularly. When I became a platelet recipient, I asked her if she could find out where her platelets ended up. She discovered that they went to DFCI and BWH, as well as other hospitals. I decided then and there that I must have received some of her platelets.

Peggy and I also have the same birthday (albeit 25 years apart). We were now officially sisters, I decided, and I immediately started calling her Sis. She tolerated it, probably because she considered me to be an eccentric old lady!

Because platelets take a long time to enter the bloodstream, I lay in bed for the entire morning. Out my window I could see a slice of gunmetal gray sky, and, around mid-morning, it started to rain. Before long it was coming down in sheets, taking me back to another rain-drenched occasion.

During the month of our wedding, I performed three other marriage services on successive Saturdays—each one the essence of a beautiful, sunlit, English April.

The following week, our wedding day dawned with torrential rain.

Joanie and I had coffee and toast together that morning, in a sisterly fashion, but that was the last quiet moment I would have all day.

I remember:

... gathering single-use cameras (no digital photography in those days), and place names for the evening reception ...

... strapping the wedding cake into the front seat of the car, with its own seatbelt ...

... Muth wandering around in the wrong part of the hotel, carrying the box of unplaced place names and Dad's freshly ironed shirt ...

... using a few choice words to Muth, while overheard by my soon-to-be in-laws, standing right behind me. Whoops! ...

... cousin Eleanor placing her hand-painted flowers on top of the wedding cake—a cake that could definitely not be left out in the rain ...

... Muth holding a golf umbrella over the cake while I retrieved it from the car ...

... screaming Dad's name from my driver's seat while he passed by, oblivious, on the sidewalk ...

... realizing I had yelled at both my parents on my wedding day.

In the middle of having my hair done, I suddenly remembered that my cousin Philip's girlfriend was a vegetarian. I called the hotel, but I waited so long for the hotel manager to come to the phone, that I finally allowed Richard, my hairdresser, to take over. As Joanie and I rushed out of the salon, me with headdress and veil in place, we could hear Richard saying, "That's right, Ann Clark, table six ... vegetarian..."

The rain had become good and earnest by then, and any hope of a dry, sunny wedding had trickled down the municipal drain. I toyed with the speed limit and we were soon home free.

My entire family, including parents, siblings, nieces, nephew, aunt, and cousins, greeted me cheerfully as I came through the door, shaking raindrops from my veil.

I raced upstairs to put on my undergarment and roll-up stockings, that immediately began rolling down. I had just zipped myself into my dressing gown, when the make-up lady arrived. We made it, by the skin of our teeth, and she made sure I didn't have lipstick on mine.

The rest of the house party had originally planned to walk to church, but the downpour meant that our friend Charles had to ferry everyone there in carloads.

Rain, rain, and more rain ...

... the parish caretaker meeting vehicles, with a large umbrella, and escorting guests up the path to the church entrance ...

... the nuptials starting ten minutes late, with an overflowing worship space full of love and good wishes ...

... being married by Rev. George, blessed by the bishop, and treated to a thoughtful sermon on radical hospitality by a clergy friend from Durham ...

... the rain stopping in time for our wedding photos to be taken outdoors ...

... Joanie's newly dyed shoes acquiring tide marks ...

... ladies of the parish hosting an afternoon reception tea in the church hall: sausage rolls, scones with jam and clotted cream, Victoria sponge, Battenberg cakes, cookies and sandwiches of all kinds. Michael and I didn't eat a single bite! ...

... a line so long for the tea service that I took someone's newly poured cup of tea right out of his hand but, being the bride, got away with it ...

... speechmaking, beginning with Michael's very sweet remarks about his new wife, then the Churchwarden, the Archdeacon of the Diocese, and me ...

... the Archdeacon's story about a bride who worried she'd forget what to do in the marriage ceremony, advised by her priest to remember just three things: 1) Come down the AISLE; 2) Stand at the ALTAR; 3) Sing a HYMN. "Aisle, altar, hymn," she repeated to herself ...

... thrusting my bouquet into the hands of a spinster of the parish, my age—who sent me an email, more than twenty years later, saying that the bouquet had finally worked. She was married at age 65! ...

... a bomb scare causing a traffic jam that held up everyone heading to the evening reception ...

... Michael and I going to our room at the end of the evening and, for the first time in our respective lives, taking a jacuzzi bath. Together...

That was not the only thing we did for the first time that night.

......

My reverie was broken as the last remaining platelets oozed into my chest and Florence came to untether me.

"You should feel a little better now," she said, cheerily.

And, funnily enough, I did.

Chapter Twenty-three: T-Day Plus Seven
"I would rather suffer with coffee than be senseless."
Napoleon Bonaparte

This morning my blood count showed a double nadir, and I was soon hooked up to baggies of both platelets and red blood cells. When my college pals started texting, bright and early, Lorrie asked me how I was.

"Bleh," I had to admit.

Lorrie responded with a little rhyme:

"Bleh, bleh, go away.
Don't come back on ANY day!"

I cannot imagine why that admonition wasn't part of my treatment plan. What a pick-me-up it would have been if my medical team were to recite it during their daily rounds. I shared this thought with my friends.

"You should teach that ditty to your doctors," Lorrie suggested.

Christine chimed in, "Monty Python doctors."

Numerous laughter emoticons popped up on the screen, and my day had begun.

Reader's Digest is right: laughter is the best medicine. Even the Bible says so:

"A cheerful heart is a good medicine..." Proverbs 17:22

Lorrie told us she would be visiting her favorite coffee shop later for a café au lait, which reminded me that I hadn't fired up my Keurig for my usual morning coffee. I felt so bleh that I didn't have energy for anything more than water.

I felt completely hollowed out—as though there were no substance to my body beyond the skin holding me together. I had stopped looking at myself in the mirror, because it was disconcerting to realize that I was both bald and haggard—but I caught a glimpse of myself this morning.

My face had a yellow tinge and my eyes had sunk into dark shadows. I looked even worse than I felt.

And I didn't even have the option of coffee to revive me. What I would have given for a cup of rich, dark, Italian coffee.

The coffee in Italy is exquisite, as Michael and I discovered on our honeymoon. We had two weeks there, beginning in Venice, where we browsed in shops full of Murano glass, had the obligatory ride in a gondola, and ate gelati in every flavor imaginable.

For the second week, we took the train to Florence. It was a hot day and we were very thirsty, but we soon discovered that there was no restaurant car. That didn't seem to matter though, because whenever we stopped at a station, the train would remain stationary for up to ten minutes—plenty of time to disembark and purchase drinks on the platform.

At the very next stop, Michael got off and went in search of Fanta.

Less than a minute later, I heard the announcement that the train was departing.

Michael hadn't returned! How could I hold the train until he got back on? I panicked and threw myself into the nearest doorway, preventing the automatic door from closing all the way, which, in turn, prevented the train from moving.

The conductor appeared, with brisk authority. "Per favore, signora," he ordered me, none too kindly, "si sieda. Adesso!" ("Please, signora, sit down. Now!")

Somehow I conjured up enough Italian to wail, "Mio marito! Mio marito!" ("My husband! My husband!")

But the doors closed, the train moved off, and I collapsed in tears. Long minutes dragged by as I sobbed and wondered how and when I would see Michael again. Should I get off the train at the next station? And what about our luggage?

Then I heard a familiar voice. "Hello," he said. It was mio marito!

After he'd dried my tears, Michael explained that he'd heard the announcement that the train was leaving and was able to reboard a few carriages down.

What? He hadn't had time to buy drinks? But I'll take a dry mouth over leaving my husband in a foreign train station any day!

Italy is supposed to be a country of love and romance. Apparently not, however—because, when we arrived at our hotel, we discovered that our room had twin beds.

Michael and I did our best to explain that it was our honeymoon, for crying out loud, and pushing the beds together, as the hotel manager suggested, was not an option. We were finally given another room: a suite with a double bed.

The time had come to shake off the ordeals of the day and make the most of beautiful Florence.

Each day began with a cup of that excellent Italian coffee. But one morning, just a few days into our stay,

I took a sip from my usually fragrant cup and found it to be awful in every way! When I asked Michael what was wrong with the coffee, he assured me that his tasted as delicious as ever. Very strange.

Back in England, the coffee problem persisted. Even the once-delicious brew from our own machine was undrinkable. What was wrong with me?

I began to have my suspicions. Since I was a local priest, and there were parishioners' eyes everywhere, I asked a friend to purchase a testing kit for me. Being over fifty at the time, she wasn't thrilled about the errand, but she did it for me, being a true friend.

It was my first time taking a home pregnancy test, but I followed the directions, and, sure enough, two little pink lines appeared.

I was pregnant! And, when we did the math, it was clear that I had conceived on our wedding night.

We hadn't intended for this to happen so soon, but we immediately started to make plans for including a little someone in our life. And we temporarily named that little someone Munchkin.

A few weeks later, Michael and I were attending a two-day conference in London, and we stayed overnight with our friends, Ashley and AJ. When we came down to breakfast, Ashley had made coffee that smelled so good, I simply had to have some ... and it was delicious.

That was how I found out we had lost Munchkin, our wedding night baby.

I was forty years old, and we both knew the odds were not in our favor for a successful pregnancy. But it was heartbreaking to lose Munchkin, along with our dreams of welcoming him or her into the world and becoming a family of three.

A colleague, who was chaplain at a local hospital, offered to conduct a memorial service for Munchkin. We were touched by her simple prayers, and by her use of that whimsical name we had given our baby-to-be, as she helped us to let go and allow God to comfort us.

We had Munchkin's name recorded in the book of remembrance in the Children's Chapel at Guildford Cathedral, a permanent reminder to go with the one etched on our hearts.

As the months went by, I was acutely aware that my biological clock was ticking. Time was passing. Eager to try again for a child, Michael and I started to keep careful track of calendar dates and my body temperature.

Michael even took a day's personal leave for us to spend the day in bed. As well as the serious work of baby-making, we watched movies, ate pizza and ice cream, and caught up on our sleep. Michael still remembers the day wistfully. But sadly, nothing came of our efforts other than a couple of extra pounds on the bathroom scale.

My honeymoon reverie, and the aching memories of the baby that never was, had the effect of crowding out that feeling of "bleh" that had overwhelmed me when I first awoke. Losing one's hair, losing one's looks, even losing one's strength; none of these begins to compare with losing one's child—or the dream of one's child.

Still, Michael and I had survived that great loss, more than once, and we would survive the much lesser setbacks I was facing now, in my daily journey to full recovery.

Diane made me a cup of coffee and it was delicious.

Chapter Twenty-four: T-Day Plus Eight
The Best Medicine

Florence had warned me to expect fever spikes and there they were, as promised, when I awoke, along with the aches that invariably accompany fevers—at least they do when I have one, which is a rare event. I still had that sense of my body being hollowed out, only now the hollow feeling was being filled with a new kind of pain.

I was receiving daily injections to stimulate cell growth in my bone marrow, and it was causing what Florence identified as bone pain. It was a grinding ache from deep inside my body—the kind of pain that you think you can get rid of by stretching or walking it off.

But nothing worked.

The worst part was the way the ache went straight to those parts of me that were already sore, which, in my case was my broken back. I was one hurting gal.

But I wasn't the only one in our college group who was dealing with pain. Robyn texted to report that she had a case of shingles. She was kicking herself because she'd been intending to get the vaccine but just hadn't gotten around to it. The group commiserated, especially those who had experienced the agony of shingles themselves.

"Poor Robyn!" Sue responded. "I remember feeling as though my skin was on fire!"

Robyn's shingles turned out to be a mild case, thank goodness, but she had learned her lesson. She got the vaccine as soon as her doctor gave her the go-ahead.

I have not had shingles, I am glad to say, and I have had the vaccine.

However, as with every vaccine I have ever received, re-vaccination would be needed once I completed my post-transplant treatment. Just another feature of being a newborn baby in an adult body: MMR, Polio, Whooping Cough, the works. Until I completed my full set of vaccinations, I'd be susceptible to any and all germs—and I would have to be especially careful about contact with our little granddaughter, Lily.

That morning at BWH, I had a new nurse, Brittany, who had not yet met me. A couple of hours after administering my morning pills, she asked me if the medication was helping my pain, and I replied, "All it's doing is waving at it."

She looked at me blankly, clearly not appreciating my attempt at humor.

I pretended to be a pain pill waving at the pain and saying "Hello!" in a cheerful fashion.

Then she got it, and realized she was allowed to laugh. I believe she realized more than that because I saw the light go on as she made the connection.

"Oh right," I could practically hear her thinking, "this is the patient who knows how to have fun even when she feels crappy."

If that were indeed what Brittany was thinking, she was absolutely right. And if someday (far in the future) my tombstone were to be engraved with words to that effect, I could not ask for a better epitaph.

......

But there are certain occasions when laughter is inappropriate.

Church services were particularly hard on my siblings and me, in our youth, because someone was invariably making someone else laugh—especially when Peter and I smuggled in a troll or two. Our parents tried separating us, to no avail; we simply carried on our antics behind their backs when they leaned forward to pray, or stood to sing.

Another unsuitable setting for childish hilarity, was the dinner table—but only when we had guests. When we dissolved into giggles at an ordinary family meal, our parents were often right there with us, but when guests were present it was a different story entirely—especially if the guests themselves were the cause of our mirth.

One summer, in the more recent past, I was attending a residential clergy conference, and the leaders decided to make one lunchtime a silent meal. A form of mindfulness, this approach is intended to focus one's mind on the look, smell, texture, and taste of the food, without the distraction of table conversation. To avoid having to listen to other diners' chewing and swallowing, music is often played at a silent meal, or someone reads aloud from the Bible or some other inspiring work.

On this occasion, our host had chosen to read a meditation on the various sources of food and drink, beginning with the streams that provided the water we were drinking.

She moved on to fields of grain, giving thanks for the farmers, harvesters, millers, and bakers. She described vegetable gardens, orchards, rice paddies, and vineyards, and gave thanks for the many workers responsible for the respective crops. Then she extolled the virtues of fresh eggs, milk, cheese, and other products of dairy animals. Finally, as she honored the creatures who gave their life to provide our food, the priest sitting across from me mimed a deep, tragic sigh, and I lost it.

It was the kind of laughter that was so much a part of my childhood: soundless exhalations invariably followed by a gasp, to refill lungs emptied of air. That gasp might also be soundless, but, on this occasion, it came out as a loud sob in an otherwise silent room. I was mortified. The woman responsible for my laughing fit managed to look both innocent and smug at the same time. I just looked like an idiot.

A similar theme featured on my first Sunday at seminary in Durham, when there was a Harvest Festival celebration at my new church. Harvest Festival is similar to our Thanksgiving, but without the connotations of escaping from the evil English. (My British father was once asked if there is a Thanksgiving Day in England, and he replied, "Yes. It's the fourth of July!")

Because there were many young families in attendance, the sermon that day took the form of a children's talk by a very earnest young woman who had brought an assortment of visual aids. She began her talk by holding up a sheaf of wheat and a farmer's loaf to illustrate "the harvest of the fields" and how it became bread. Next, she talked about "the harvest of the seas," handing out real (dead) fish that the children gleefully brandished up and down the aisles and handed to horrified parents. "The harvest of the hedgerows and woodlands" dragged on a bit as she described numerous varieties of berry, then we went on to vegetables and fruit ("the harvest of the land").

We all listened gratefully to the relative merits of parsnips, leeks, and pineapples, in anticipation of the closing message. Instead, a lump of coal was produced, along with an enthusiastic discourse on "the harvest from under the earth." At this point, the woman next to me was heard to mutter, "She'll be bringing out a chunk of uranium next!"

I nearly laughed out loud. In fact, if I hadn't been new to the congregation, I probably would have. Although I didn't know it at the time, my future husband was sitting in the pew behind me. He told me later that he too had stifled a giggle.

As I contended with bone pain, fever, gastric distress, and that infernal weakness, laughter might have been severely lacking on T-Day plus eight. But, once again, memories had come to the rescue.

And then Diane came into my room singing Good Morning, Starshine. Daisy's shout, "I'm GOOD," shook the rafters. And Brittany laughed at my joke about the pain meds waving at my pain and saying, "Hello!"

It hurt to laugh, but it would have hurt so much more not to.

Chapter Twenty-five: T-Day Plus Nine
Sea Changes

At some point during the night, my fever had apparently broken, causing me to wake up drenched in sweat.

A baggie of antibiotics had been added to Bernie the previous day, to treat whatever had caused my elevated temperature. According to Florence, the doctors don't always know what causes the post-transplant fever spike. It could be any number of incipient infections, she said, and, since something almost always does show up, they were prepared to treat it with a broad-spectrum antibiotic. It seemed to have done the trick.

I still struggled with the omnipresent diarrhea, plus full-body pain from the bone marrow stimulant, but I took any and all side effects as good signs. After all, side effects, by definition, exist next to the main effect: that my healthy cells were multiplying and spreading. I may not have been feeling great, but that's because I was being cured. I'll take it!

My friend Sue shared some heartening news in our morning text chat. After losing their mother the previous year, she and her brother had spent several weeks recently preparing to put the family home up for sale. They cleared out the furniture and other contents, and Sue was giving the piano to a music teacher whose own instrument was irreparable. She had also promised the sleeper sofa to a Venezuelan immigrant family and was trying to figure out how to get it to them. When the mover arrived that day to transport the piano to its new home, he offered to deliver—free of charge—the sleeper sofa, and other odds and ends, to the refugee family!

Sue was delighted, and so grateful. She commented to our group how touched people are when they hear about a family, with two children, who walked for months through horrendous conditions, to reach the safety of this country. "Just a few new neighbors can help get them settled," she observed.

Kindness is a ministry, and Sue's mover was a prime example. So was Sue.

Like many city center faith communities, St. Cat's was involved in a number of outreach ministries, including the "Family Promise" program. The goal of Family Promise is to provide food and shelter for temporarily homeless families, while helping them find permanent housing and employment.

The assistance with job applications and home-hunting takes place in a day center, where unemployed parents and under-school-age children spend their days in the company of case workers. The overnight accommodation and meals are provided by local churches, synagogues, and mosques, who take turns housing and feeding the families, for a week at a time, four times a year.

In the few rules for participation in Family Promise, the main one requires applicants to be some configuration of a family. What that means is, whatever the circumstances of the adults, there must be children involved.

St. Cat's was hosting two families one wintry week. One of them was a single mother and her four children. The morning after their second night with us, I had to go into the room they were using to retrieve something from a storage closet. The family had gone for the day—the kids to school and Mom to the day center—and they had left their room in apple pie order. All five of the beds were carefully made; there was nothing on the floor that didn't belong there; and lined up neatly on a clean washcloth on a table, were five toothbrushes and a tube of tooth-paste. Not only was that young mother taking good care of their temporary home, she was teaching her children the values she lived by.

As the week wore on there were many more instances of her good parenting, and I was not surprised, a month later, to hear that she had found a job, and the family had moved into an apartment.

It's all too easy to make assumptions about people experiencing homelessness. The reality is that a single, unexpected occurrence can set into motion a chain of events that causes an individual or a family to lose their home. An unexpected illness or injury; a job loss; a relationship breakdown; a *vehicle* break-down... there are numerous incidents which can trigger a catastrophic change of circumstances. Family Promise recognizes this and works to help put right what has gone wrong.

One year, the week before Christmas, a young couple came to St. Cat's seeking assistance. They had been living in a homeless camp on the edge of town, when there was a heavy snowfall overnight. Their tent had collapsed under the weight of snow and was unusable. The weather was frigid, more snow was forecast, and they had nowhere to go.

Because there were no children involved, we couldn't help the couple through the Family Promise program, but I was able to use my discretionary fund to put them up in a hotel for a couple of nights. I then sent out an email to the parish asking for two things: 1) donations that would enable me to pay for more nights in the hotel, and 2) people willing to prepare and deliver evening meals for the couple, for as long as they were in the hotel.

The couple also had a case worker at the local homeless resource center, who was in the process of getting them a replacement tent, sleeping bags, stove, and other items that would make them safer and more comfortable when they returned to the camp.

Thanks to the generosity of St. Cat's parishioners, the couple was able to stay in the hotel, and be fed daily with a hot meal, over Christmas and New Year, and well into January.

For faith communities involved in the Family Promise program, and for the individuals who delivered home-cooked meals or helped pay the hotel bill for that unfortunate couple, these were opportunities to gain a new perspective, to understand that homeless people are rarely any different from people settled in stable accommodation—they are simply unlucky.

I have often thought that the path from judgment to acceptance is one of the most life-changing journeys we can take, and one of the most powerful catalysts for the healing of division. And the healing of division is what is sorely needed in our angry and broken world.

The Episcopal Church changed its canons in 1976, allowing women to be ordained to the priesthood beginning on January 1, 1977. My grandmother—Mimi to us—was ordained that year at the age of 78, having completed seminary, and served as deacon, before the priesthood was even an option for her.

It took another 17 years for the Church of England to make the change, and I began my training a year later.

During that first year in England, hundreds of women who had already attended seminary—some many years previously—and were fully qualified, were ordained in dozens of joyous ceremonies throughout the country. I attended one such service at Guildford Cathedral in the spring of 1994, and the faces of those new priests, as they cascaded down the aisle, rivaled the sunlight that was pouring into the worship space on that glorious day.

But not everyone agreed with the decision, in the USA or in England. I encountered resentment, intolerance, and downright rudeness both during my years of preparation for ordination and beyond. And I was shocked to discover that many of the people who were opposed to women priests were themselves women!

Shortly after I started my curacy at St. Simeon's, an envelope arrived in the parish office, containing six months' worth of empty weekly offering envelopes. They were accompanied by a curt note: "I will no longer be supporting or attending St. Simeon's."

The next day, Rev. George and I paid a visit to the woman who had written the note.

When she answered the door, she didn't even look at me, but led us both into a small reception hall that had no chairs. There she stood, with her back to me, and told my rector, "I simply cannot be a part of a parish with a female curate." She added the name of the parish where she would be worshipping instead. She then dismissed us by holding open the front door and saying goodbye to George—but not to me.

It seemed like what might have been a case of divine retribution a few months later, when the church she moved to hired a female vicar.

Whether the issue is immigration, homelessness, female clergy, or something else (and there are plenty of issues to choose from), I often find that a change of perspective occurs when someone moves from a principle to a person. I wish I had a dollar for every time someone told me they'd been opposed to women priests until they met me, or one of my female colleagues. As for the genuine hospitality that was shown to our Family Promise guests, and to our friends in the hotel, this was a clear indication of minds and hearts being changed through human connection.

Kindness is a ministry. So is acceptance.

Chapter Twenty-six: T-Day Plus Ten
Bad Hair Day

Today my hair fell out.

There wasn't much there to fall out, but when my hairdresser, Tony, shaved my head, he'd left around a quarter of an inch of hair. This morning it detached from my scalp in a single mat—like a piece of gray felt. I was left with a shiny pate and a few stray hairs.

Two weeks previously, while I'd been seated in Tony's chair, draped in one of his sixties-style capes, he had carefully wrapped rubber bands around a dozen pony tails, which he cut off and put in a zip-lock bag. This was the hair I would send to the cancer wig organization.

Then he got to work with his shaver. It took him less than five minutes to shave off what was left, but Tony stopped several times to ask if I were okay.

I always was okay, and I wondered why he was being so solicitous.

And then it hit me. Tony knew that many people in my position—cancer patients undergoing treatment —were apprehensive about what they might lose. Freedom is an obvious loss, with several months of restricted activity following a stem cell transplant, but every patient has their own set of concerns. Hair loss, Tony knew from experience, is a big one for many cancer patients, who sometimes weep as their hair is clipped away.

Tony had been pausing his shaver and checking on me, just in case I had started to cry.

The truth was, losing my hair didn't bother me in the slightest. I'd always been curious to know what my head looked like without hair, and this was my chance. I had no plans to wear a wig, or a turban, or any head-covering, for that matter, unless it were necessary for protection from the sun.

After becoming hairless, most of the time I didn't—and still don't—even think about my absence of hair.

Sometimes I do have the shock of identity, however. When I catch sight of a little old bald lady in some reflective surface, I think for a moment... Wait, who is that?

And then I realize, with acceptance, it's me.

That's how it felt from the moment Tony first gave me my buzz cut—for which, by the way, he didn't charge me.

There was, however, a loss I experienced that bothered me considerably, and that was the continued absence of my appetite. My weight was carefully monitored at BWH. Every morning, a nurse would wheel a scale into my room and make a note of the numbers. And every day those numbers crept down a little more.

My lack of desire to eat was maddening. And no wonder—because what food I did manage to force down, tasted like sawdust.

When Michael made his weekly visit that Saturday, he arrived, masked and gloved, as usual, bearing my week's worth of clothing. He also produced a pack of English muffins, and a jar of orange marmalade with ginger. He'd remembered that, back when I first realized I could no longer face an omelet for breakfast, I had ordered a toasted English muffin instead. It had arrived in a foil bag, soggy, cold, and inedible.

Michael guessed that, with my own supply of muffins, and the ward's toaster, I just might manage a palatable breakfast. It was definitely worth a try.

......

My sister Joanie had come to see me the previous day, and had entered wearing a large, hastily drawn toothy grin on her face mask. She looked like Hannibal Lecter in The Silence of the Lambs—which meant that she made me laugh before the door had even closed behind her.

Joanie and I have spent much of our adult lives in the same places. For a memorable two years, we shared my house in Surrey, England, laughing our way through late night raids on the kitchen—we called them "toast fests" and "cereal murder."

We also invented a unique version of Scrabble, which added a tasty dimension to the game. On every word or letter bonus square, we placed an m&m. The lucky person landing on any of those squares was entitled to eat the m&m.

Our other innovation was to allow players to consult the Scrabble Dictionary before placing letters on the board. In other words, we cheated—but so did our mother and father before us, and it made for gratifyingly high scores.

While Joanie was visiting, I'd brought up a favorite mutual memory, about the occasion when someone broke into our house while we were in it.

During the time Joanie lived with me in Surrey, two of our friends, Andy and his twin brother Kevin, often hung out at our place. Since their other favorite hangout was the local pub, they'd often show up at the house under the influence.

One night, long after Joanie and I had gone to bed, something woke me. There was a small room beyond my bedroom, that had a window overlooking the backyard. I was pretty sure the sound had come from there. Then I heard breathing.

I tiptoed into Joanie's room and woke her up. "Someone's in the house!" I whispered. It sounded like a horror movie. But someone *was* in the house.

Joanie grabbed her softball bat and followed me.

As we reached the back room, we saw a dark figure standing in front of the window.

"Run!" I screamed at Joanie. She did, but in her panic, she started out running like a cartoon—with her legs pedaling in thin air and not going anywhere.

We were halfway down the stairs when I realized that the dark figure was our pal, Kevin. He had evidently thought it would be funny to climb through a second story window and scare the daylights out of his friends. A   skinful of beer had utterly convinced him.

Now Joanie and I were utterly convinced he needed to go home... through the front door.

After Joanie decided to move back to the States, I officially became a "spinster." A "spinster cat lady" even, because I had two of them.

The children next door often looked at me the way my siblings and I used to look, with suspicion and fear, at certain neighbors who lived alone with their cats. What imaginations we had!

At BWH the following day, Michael and I broke out the Yahtzee game which we played without cheating.

The two games of Yahztee and Scrabble were my favorites, and those two years living with Joanie were some of the happiest times of my life.

My years with Michael are some of the happiest, too.

My sister and my husband were there when I needed them. They love this little, old, bald woman, and I love them right back.

I can't imagine life without them.

Chapter Twenty-seven: T-Day Plus Eleven
Semi-Addled

Robyn was up early, preparing a couple more song title quizzes for the rest of us. When I tuned in, Ashley had already identified number one, which was Everybody's Talkin', made famous by Harry Nilsson. The next one was still up for grabs.

Me: Number two is on the tip of my texting finger... Nope, I just can't squeeze it out of the depths of my memory. It's there though, thumbing its nose at me. Any chance of another wee clue?

Robyn: The woman's name in the title of the song is both a color and a gemstone. And her name is part of the lyric that follows this one.

Me: Is there a weekday in the song title?

Robyn: Nope, but there's word similar to city.

Me: I'm on the verge of Googling, and I really don't want to do that.

Robyn: Don't give up! I'm working on another clue!

Me: Suddenly, surprising even myself, I shouted it. "Ruby, don't take your love to town!"

Robyn: You got it!!!! Yahooeee!

Me: Phew! It just suddenly and nonchalantly showed up in my addled brain.

Robyn: Your brain is anything but addled, if you ask me!

Robyn was being kind, because the truth is, my brain was addled. There is a condition known as "Chemo

Brain," and—after six months of infusions, a week-long mega-dose, and a stem cell transplant, I definitely had it. And, since my cancer was diagnosed soon after I'd contracted the Corona virus, I had Chemo Brain on top of COVID Brain. It's a wonder I could string two thoughts together.

A particularly annoying symptom of Chemo (and COVID) Brain is vocabulary drain. Most people have had the experience of suddenly forgetting the name of a person they know perfectly well—often when they're expected to introduce that person to someone else. It's very embarrassing, but it's a fleeting malfunction.

I was once in the middle of a long, involved introduction of someone I was calling Margaret, when my friend pointed out that "Margaret" was wearing a nametag that read "Dorothy."

With Chemo Brain, blunders can occur on a regular basis with names, dates, adjectives, and nouns. The word "thingamabob" comes into regular use, as does the apologetic "Sorry, Chemo Brain," and most people—certainly the BWH folks—understand.

On this occasion, a nurse came in to hang a new baggie on Bernie and fuss with the tubing. She also gave me my meds and updated my medical record. The whole time she was in my room, I chatted away with her as if we were old friends. Then, as she was leaving, she turned and said, "Violet says hi."

But I had thought that she was Violet!

Chemo brain doesn't seem to affect one's long-term memories, fortunately, because my memories played a major part in passing the time and keeping me somewhat sane.

Joanie's recent visit sparked nostalgia for that little house we had shared for two years.

In all, I spent ten happy years there, sometimes with housemates, sometimes on my own. It was a typical semi-detached (Brit-speak for two-family) Victorian, built to house railroad workers, and was identical to nearly every other house on that side of the street—none of which had off-street parking (probably because Victorian railroad workers did not generally own their own vehicles).

Behind the house was a large recreational field, owned by the town, to which I had access via a gate at the end of my backyard. I taught my cricket-playing British friends the rudiments of softball, and we would often play a few innings on the field. Andy and Kevin had been on their school's cricket team, and never got out of the habit of holding the softball bat pointing downwards!

When I left for seminary, I rented the house to a family, whose father was an amateur car mechanic. After they moved out, I was horrified to discover that he'd built a ramp leading into my back yard from the field, taken down the rear fence panels, built a carport where there once had been a flower garden, and sprayed car parts with grease on the dining room carpet (which still bore the imprints of a crankshaft, pistons, bearings, and various other pieces I could not name).

Upstairs, there had a been a leak of some description, which this man had attempted to repair by removing a large number of bathroom tiles, leaving an enormous hole in the wall. Apparently, he had not noticed the (very obvious) plumbing access panel in the adjoining room...

My lovely little house had become a shambles, but the people of St. James Church came out in force to put it right. They re-tiled the bathroom, re-painted every room, dismantled the carport, restored the fence panels and replaced the dining room carpet. It was as good as new, although I would never live there again. Another family of renters took possession shortly after I moved into the curate's house provided by St. Simeon's.

My church house had been purchased some years previously for another single curate. It originally had only two bedrooms, one of which was used as a study. Because it was not deemed appropriate for parishioners to go upstairs for meetings with the priest, a study was being added to the ground floor of the house, with two more bedrooms above it.

Although I'd been a single woman when I was first offered my curacy, I had become "a little less single," as I described it to Rev. George, in the interim. It would be nice for Michael and me to have the extra space after we were married, which I fully expected us to be before the year was out.

Rev. George had a different opinion, as it happened. Because he had been involved in a failed long-distance relationship when he was eighteen, he assured me that Michael and I would be breaking up before too long. Clearly, he was wrong—and I admit to hoping we'll run into him again someday so we can gloat.

Construction work was still in progress when I moved into the house. Consequently, I became used to opening the door to a variety of noisy builders, electricians, plumbers, and painters. They were there on my days off as well, so it was several months before I could have the luxury of sleeping late.

After Michael proposed to me at the kitchen sink, and I burst out laughing, a plumber working in the bathroom upstairs came running down to see what was so funny.

One's life is rarely one's own in the Church!

And one's life is certainly not one's own in the hospital. What with flapping johnnies, fluid input and output measurement, unbridled diarrhea, and necessary assistance in the shower, my only option was to leave my dignity on the bus. Perhaps it helped that I was somewhat addled, because it stopped me thinking too much about what was happening to me.

What has stuck in my mind was the nursing staff's kind, matter-of-fact, nonjudgmental response to my needs—no matter how personal or intimate those needs may have been.

It takes a special kind of angel to be a cancer nurse.

Chapter Twenty-eight: T-Day Plus Twelve
Crossroads

It was time for my daily visit from Drs. Chen and Miller, accompanied by the ever-vigilant Florence. I immediately noticed something different about my medical team. Even the stern Dr. Miller had an air of levity about her. Then all became clear.

"You're finished with the antibiotics," she began, "and you're drinking enough to make IV fluids unnecessary. Your white blood cell count this morning is nearly double yesterday's. The pneumonia has been successfully treated and your lungs are clear." She almost smiled, "and I see that you have been reporting much lower numbers on the pain scale for your back."

I had a hint of what was about to happen.

"It looks to us like you are ready to go home."

Then she really did smile. "How about tomorrow?"

Tomorrow?

In truth I was ready.

But I was also apprehensive about conditions at home.

Michael had done all he could do in order to create a safe environment for me. He'd had the carpets steam-cleaned, and a team was coming in later that day to sanitize the kitchen and bathrooms—that is, as close to sanitized as was possible in a house with a dog and a cat.

Of course, our dog and cat were themselves health hazards. How on earth was I going to stop Ernie jumping all over me, and licking my face? And Charlie's regular contact with his litter box meant no contact with me.

Michael would have to take precautions, too. He could dispense with using latex gloves as long as he washed or sanitized his hands frequently, but he would have to wear a mask whenever he was near me.

It would be up to Michael to prepare my meals for me, following a multi-paged set of guidelines for what I could and could not eat. My "forbidden food" list was long: no berries, raw cauliflower or broccoli, raw honey, deli meats, bakery or take-out food, sushi, soft cheeses, raw nuts... anything uncooked that may have been handled by someone other than Michael, or that had a texture that might attract bacteria. It was a daunting litany.

Michael's signature dish is baked chicken with rice and salad—the meal he prepared for our first date— and that's because it's his only dish. Now he was going to be responsible for feeding the two of us, without relying on deli or hot bar foods, his usual go-to for a little variety. Either we were going to be eating a lot of baked chicken, or he was going to have to call in reinforcements.

He called in reinforcements.

The reinforcements were Dave and his wife Shelly, who were members of St. Cat's.

Dave happened to have a background in both catering and medical care. He had retired, and he and Shelly had started a business looking after pets and maintaining lawns. Now their business would be to look after Michael and me.

Michael gave Dave a copy of my food dos and don'ts, and they agreed a date for Dave to come and cook while I remained sequestered upstairs. Stem cell transplant or not, my hubby and I were going to be well fed.

I was glad to see that only raw broccoli was forbidden. Raw or cooked, broccoli is my favorite vegetable.

During my time at seminary, the vegetables in the dining hall tended to be carrots and potatoes, so overcooked that they both ended up the same beige color. I would often walk into town to buy bunches of fresh broccoli, which I would steam lightly and store in the dorm fridge, helping myself from time to time. That fresh, green broccoli was as much a treat for me as a candy bar or a cookie, and a whole lot healthier.

Nearly thirty years later, between the two of them, Michael and Dave were going to ensure that the Atkinson household got the nutrition it needed. No beige vegetables!

Michael would have to take on a number of tasks that were not his usual responsibility. For one thing, he had to sanitize the bathroom regularly. Since it was still recommended that I change clothes daily, he would have numerous loads of laundry to do. And, because I would not be permitted to eat meals prepared outside our home, the kitchen had to be immaculate for Dave to work his culinary magic.

The last time I had been utterly dependent on Michael, was four years previously, after I had a fall in our kitchen—or should I say, my first fall in our kitchen? I was wearing socks but no shoes, which caused me to slip and land on my butt. Using both hands to break my fall, instead I broke my wrists. Both of them. Oh, and I had a fractured vertebra—or should I say, my first fractured vertebra?

As a result of that fall, I had plates inserted in both wrists and had to wear a back brace for two months. I managed pretty well with those temporary debilities, but one thing I could not do was fasten my bra. That was Michael's job, and he excelled at it— apart from the day he put it on me upside-down.

Thankfully, my post-transplant state of health did not call for assistance with dressing.

But I was still as weak as a baby. And I had been given strict instructions not to engage in any activity that would put me in contact with dirt or germs. Michael had his work cut out for him.

Still, I was going home at last!

Chapter Twenty-nine: T-Day Plus Thirteen
There's No Place Like Home

Before leaving BWH, I had to have the central line removed from my chest by a surgical team of two that came to my room. One of them, Lance, was an incredibly tall, lanky, young Black man. The other was Rose, a very short, round, middle-aged Asian woman. Add me, an average-sized elderly white lady, and we were our own little microcosm of diversity.

As Rose began listing the steps to be taken, it became clear that Lance was in training, and Rose was his supervisor. Judging by the detail of her instructions, it also became clear that mine was the first central line removal Lance had ever performed. Yet he was so focused, careful, and measured in his movements, that I trusted him completely. Rose was an excellent coach: patient, supportive, and quick to assist, but only when Lance asked for her help. Despite a height disparity of nearly two feet, they were a great pair.

One aspect of the procedure proved challenging. Because of Lance's great height, my bed had to be raised to its highest level. Even then, Lance had to crouch down to do his work. Rose, on the other hand, could barely reach the site. For one tricky part of the process, when two pairs of hands were needed, the bed had to go back down again—and Lance was practically bent double.

He took out the sutures holding the line in place, and then came the main event. The tube extended approximately four inches, under my skin, into my upper chest. The best way to remove it was to yank.

"Take a big breath," Lance instructed, while Rose took hold of my hand.

"Now blow it out!"

I blew, Lance pulled, and my dingles were no longer dangling. I wish I could say it was painless, but that would be a lie.

Lance dressed the hole in my chest with a pressure bandage and gave me instructions about keeping the area dry and refraining from heavy lifting.

And then they were ready to depart.

But first I had to channel Muth and tell Lance what a good doctor he was going to be. As he ducked his head to go out the door, he broke into a big grin and I could tell he was pleased—both with the success of his debut and with my remark. Rose was beaming like a proud mother.

A few more things had to be done before I would be free to go. I had an extensive list of medications that Florence had taken me through in detail. She even noted on the pill bottle labels what each one was for: anti-nausea tablets, prophylactic antibiotics, folic acid, magnesium, vitamins, bone-strengtheners, and shingles prevention pills.

But at least nothing was dripping into my veins anymore. I was untethered. I would soon be free.

First, I had to pack.

I emptied Kate's Kitchen of its trusty kettle and coffee maker. I bundled together a week's worth of daily wardrobe changes. I packed English muffins, cans of Diet Coke, pudding cups, and packets of oyster crackers into my pink plastic wash tub, which would have been thrown away if I hadn't taken it home—and what a handy item it was. I also filled my backpack with all the books and magazines I hadn't read, the crossword puzzles I hadn't done, the coloring books I hadn't colored, and the Scrabble and Yahtzee games I had played.

Just enough space was left for my ten bottles of pills.

I was dressed and I was packed, just waiting for my husband and the car to take me home.

Michael arrived in the early afternoon, and Florence brought my discharge papers so that she could go through them again with both of us. Then she loaded me and my wash tub into a wheelchair, and pushed me out into the hall. Michael followed, dragging my suitcase and wrangling a helium "Get Well Soon" balloon that kept floating into his face.

Diane came over to say goodbye—not singing this time—and Missy came out of a patient's room just in time to add her farewell. But no one else was around, so it was a quiet departure, very different from the raucous exchanges that had taken place in my room over the previous three weeks.

Florence helped me into the car's passenger seat while Michael loaded the trunk—and weighed down the unruly balloon. Just before we drove off, Florence slipped something into the pocket of my sweatshirt and gave me a quick, illegal hug.

We were on our way!

Boston's traffic was atrocious, but the sun was shining, I was sitting in a car with my Michael, and I would soon be home. Life was sweet.

As we drove onto the highway, I reached into my pocket for Florence's parting gift.

She had given me the Starfish Award.

......

When we arrived at the house, Ernie was napping in his playpen, but he roused himself when he heard the door open. I swear that pup did a double-take! When he realized it was me, he got up on his hind legs, and started scrabbling at his enclosure, barking like a mad dog. Michael got him out, and it was all we could do to stop him licking my face; Ernie was beside himself—and so was I.

Then Charlie made an appearance, sauntering into the kitchen and acting as though my three-week absence had been no big deal. But he couldn't fool me. From the other side of the room, I could hear him purring like a V-8 engine.

It was a wonderful feeling to be with my beloved husband and our dear animals again. Yet, I also felt a little overwhelmed. I'd been kept so safe in my BWH room, with its noisy air exchange and mask and glove precautions. Now it was up to Michael and me to protect myself from harm—a heavy responsibility for us both.

For the rest of that day, I sat perched on a kitchen chair, afraid to be in contact with any upholstery that might be harboring germs.

Being back in that kitchen felt so comfortable and familiar. And those were feelings I recognized from years before we even lived in the house, because I used to visit the previous owner, Joan, an elderly woman who was a homebound member of my parish.

A brain tumor had caused Joan to lose her sight before I met her, and her favorite place to spend her days was in the peaceful sunroom attached to a beautiful kitchen. Joan had supervised the addition of that space thirty years earlier, choosing stunning tiger maple woodwork and large windows looking out on the garden she had also designed. She could no longer see the beauty she had created, but she could still experience the sense of peace it inspired.

As I spent time with Joan, on several occasions, in that lovely, serene setting, I often felt that I was the one who gained most from the visits.

But it was becoming increasingly difficult for Joan to live on her own, and she eventually moved into a nursing home. She died three years later.

Shortly after Joan's funeral, I passed her house as I drove Alex to her first day of high school.

A "For Sale" sign stood in the front yard.

As soon as I had dropped off Alex, I called our realtor, who took the three of us to view the house that same afternoon. Michael and Alex both gave their seal of approval. Two months later, the house was ours.

Even crammed with movers' boxes, and the upheaval of new appliances, the sunroom had that same feeling of peace I'd experienced years earlier, sitting with a lonely woman who could no longer see the beauty she'd created.

Our house is still a peaceful oasis in a chaotic world, and I was so glad to be home.

Chapter Thirty: T-Day Plus Fourteen
Sticking Around

On my first full day back home, I slept well into the morning, due to all the excitement and exertions of the previous day. I woke up to a flurry of messages from my college pals. Sue texted, "Did you sleep well? It must have been nice to wake up in your own bed."

It certainly had been wonderful to wake up in my own home, although I wouldn't be in my own bed for some time. That was part of my recovery plan: to make sure that I was kept as safe as possible from wayward germs, Michael and I would be sleeping in separate rooms, at least until I reached the critical thirty days post-transplant.

I would be using the guest bathroom as well—which had the added benefit of getting Michael off the hook of daily cleaning. We still needed to be ultra careful, of course. Along with keeping the bathroom clean, Michael had to wash my towels, sheets, and sleepwear twice a week, and keep on top of the rest of my laundry.

Michael's newly-extended to-do list, on top of a full-time job, proved to be somewhat more than he could handle, despite the fact that he worked from home (and what a blessing that was!). It didn't take long for the   laundry room floor to accumulate piles of clothing, and the kitchen sink to be filled with a mass of pots and pans.

Joanie came to the rescue. She arrived for a visit, and spent the day washing the dishes, cleaning the kitchen, and doing four loads of laundry. "Do you have any firewood you need split?" she quipped as she scrubbed. My sister is the best!

Michael is no slouch, however, in being helpful in important ways, and he was so transparently delighted to have his wife home again, that I was quick to forgive him his lapses when it came to housework. I was reminded, as I have been regularly throughout 26 years of marriage, that his claim, "I can never leave the washing-up," made on that long-ago first date, was at the very least, an exaggeration.

Still, if Michael had told me he was a slob, I might not have gone out with him, and that would have been my great loss.

One of the texts, that particular morning, was from Lorrie. "Today is 'International Tiara Day,' ladies," she announced. "So be sure to wear your tiaras."

It just so happens that I own a tiara, and it was Michael's job to find it in the costume box. But first he had to find the costume box in the basement. I couldn't help him because one of my going-home instructions was to stay out of the basement, due to the health dangers of dust and mold.

All I could do was shout out directions to Michael while he stared at the shelves in the storage room.

He reminded me of a cartoon I once saw in The New Yorker: A husband is standing in front of an open fridge packed with nothing but boxes of butter. In the caption, he asks, "Honey, do we have any butter?"

That's what Michael is like when he's looking for something. We call it "seeing a morass," which was what he was doing in the basement.

Eventually he found the box, and retrieved the tiara buried under other dress-up clothes for grown-ups. A photo of me wearing it on my bald head was soon winging its way to the rest of the gang—triggering another flurry of texts:

"Love the look!"

"Royally impressed."

"Trust Kate to rock baldness!"

It felt so good to be back in the house that I loved, surrounded by objects that gave me joy.

Still, an unexpected emotion cropped up that day. Somehow, being away for three weeks then returning home to be with my beloved husband and animals, triggered powerful memories of my parents.

Perhaps it was the wave of affection for a special home they had never seen and would have loved.

Or maybe because I was contending with a serious disease and treatment, it brought to mind my mother's courage and forbearance with her own health challenges.

Whatever the cause, I experienced a wave of nostalgia for my parents so overwhelming that it made me weep.

Dad and Muth, officially known as Guy and Jill, had met in kind of a miraculous way—as if in a movie. The setting was Brussels, 1952.

Although my father was an Englishman, he had been born in Belgium and had lived there until he was thirteen years old, when his family was forced, by Hitler, to escape to Britain. Twelve years later, after qualifying as a civil engineer, he took a job in Brussels.

Jill was born and raised in Madison, Wisconsin, the daughter of a clergyman and his scholarly wife. She was an adventurous twenty-five-year-old, happy to pull up her mid-western roots and see the world. She, too, was working in Brussels, as a secretary for the American Embassy.

They didn't meet because of their work, however. They met because they were both interested in acting, and both tried out for parts in an amateur dramatics group. On the evening of the auditions, Jill invited several of the aspiring actors to an impromptu after-party at her apartment. The wannabe actors were American and British expatriates, and several of them already knew one another. But the tall, red-haired Englishman was new to the group, and he had caught Jill's eye.

At the end of the evening, as her guests were collecting their coats, Jill stage-whispered "Stick around" to that one particular guest, Guy.

And he did.

Two weeks after that momentous invitation, Guy said, "I love you" to Jill.

"So," Jill replied, "what are you going to do about it?"

"Marry you?" he guessed.

They were married, by Jill's father, in her parents' new hometown, Tulsa, Oklahoma. Overseas travel was prohibitive in those days, so they dispensed with the "Bride's" and "Groom's" sides of the church.

Otherwise Guy's side would have been completely empty!

They both stuck around for nearly 60 years of marriage and four boisterous children together, and the story of the beginning of their romance was a favorite of us all.

And how did the auditions turn out?

Muth was proud to say, "I got the part, but he got the girl!"

When each of my siblings and I reached age thirteen, our parents would rent a hall and throw a birthday party for us, with dance music. Most of our friends, at that age, would have parties without adults present, which would include various types of experimentation—such as cigarettes, kissing, and Mateus Rosé. But our parents were fully present. Not only that, but Dad made us play games. No spin-the-bottle or sardines-in-the-dark; Dad organized teams for balloon volleyball, and had us pass lifesavers to each other, on the end of straws, without dropping them. We danced too, but he would make us freeze when he stopped the music—and the last one standing still would win a prize.

All four of us, in succession, begged our father to let us have a party like everyone else's, but he stood firm.

Our classmates talked about those parties for days afterwards, saying that each one was the best party ever. Dad knew what he was doing—and he was going to make sure our teenage years began with some good, old-fashioned fun. After all, his kids would be having plenty of the other kind of fun as time went on, and Dad's games would merge into happy childhood memories.

In a loving family, like mine, it's natural to hope our parents will stay the same—or at least not change much as they get older. But illness can rob them, and us. Alzheimers is a cruel disease.

Dad was in his early 70s when we began to notice changes—objects left in nonsensical places, repetition of things he'd said just a few minutes before, and strange word choices, like comb for phone or movie for store. At dinner one visit, I mentioned the name of a dear family friend, and he had no idea who I was talking about. That was when we knew something was very wrong.

Dad and Muth had been avid bridge players; on one occasion they even played in a tournament in which Omar Sharif was a competitor—at a much higher level, but still—and Dad retained his card skills well into his illness. He had also loved to do jigsaw puzzles with 1,000 or more pieces. He took up solitaire on the computer when he was already showing signs of cognitive failure.

Bridge went first, then solitaire. And in the final year of his illness, although he was still doing jigsaws, they were children's puzzles, with a dozen pieces or so, and he would assemble the same one over and over again. It was heartbreaking to witness.

In the earlier years of his illness, Dad would take daily walks—often five miles or more—until he reached the stage when he would get lost as soon as he left the assisted living home they had moved to. His body remained strong to the end, but his wonderful mind, his inimitable sense of humor, and his familiar stories of long ago, had by that time all slipped away.

Although Muth was sharp as a tack to the day she died, she had to contend with physical challenges. She used to say she had arthritis "everywhere except my hair." And multiple myeloma caused excruciating pain in all the bones of her body. It was more and more difficult for her to move in her final days, but nothing stopped her engaging fully with life.

Muth died in September, 2010. Dad followed her the day after the New Year 2011.

As I settled back into the lovely house they never saw, my mind was full of memories and my heart was full of sorrow. I still miss them every day.

Chapter Thirty-one: T-Day Plus Fifteen
Alex

The day started early with a phone call from our daughter Alex—who often called before 7:00, having been awake for an hour or more with her toddler, Lily. I hadn't heard from her for a while, but that's how it was with Alex: long silences followed by spates of daily phone calls—often video calls with Lily. We were watching our granddaughter grow up on the screen of a cellphone.

We adopted Alex through Surrey Social Services, in England, when she was eleven months old. She was the second daughter of her birth mother, who then went on to give birth to two boys and another girl, a total of five children from four different fathers. Alex was the only one of the five to be adopted outside the family; her elder sister, and the brother born less than a year after Alex, were both brought up by their grandparents. The other brother and sister stayed with their mother, who eventually married their father and had her tubes tied.

From the time Alex first came to us, we worried that she might struggle with the circumstances of her adoption, when she was old enough to understand them.

Michael and I longed for a family, and, because we were willing to adopt a sibling pair, one of whom hadn't been born yet, we were permitted to have infants, despite my great age of 43. But Alex's birth mother left the county less than a month before her son was born, and, since the family was no longer under the jurisdiction of Surrey Social Services, there was nothing we could do. The baby boy's grandmother (who is five years younger than I) was granted guardianship of him, and Alex became our only child.

Alex was the light of our life. She woke up happy every morning, and would come into our room and pretend to be an egg under the bedsheet. It was our job to guess what kind of baby animal was in the egg—and it didn't matter in the slightest that the animals Alex chose were usually not oviparous. Her favorite was a kitten.

From an early age, Alex loved music. Her foster family had been members of an evangelical church, where it was common for congregants to lift their hands in the air when singing praise songs. As a result, whenever Alex heard music—whether it was Rock of Ages or Mary Had a Little Lamb—she would raise her hands. And, on road trips, her little voice, coming from the car seat behind us, would regularly request "la-la," her term for music.

We called Alex a "credit dancer" because, at the end of every movie we watched as a family, Alex would spring out of her seat and dance to the music that played while the credits rolled. At the age of nine, she started going to dance classes, and had soon mastered tap and hip-hop. As a result, every December and June, Michael and I would sit through a three-hour recital to watch our daughter dance for two minutes.

Alex was a world traveler by the time she reached her teens. While we were still living in England, it was only a short hop across the Channel to Europe, and she had even visited the West Coast of the U.S.A. before she was two years old. Once we'd moved to the

States, just before her third birthday, the traveling continued. Before long, she'd taken several flights as an unaccompanied minor. She took part in a Spanish exchange with her high school class when she was fifteen. She even spent a summer with her godmother's family in Australia and traveled to Fiji with them.

From the age of five, Alex would occasionally accompany me on pastoral visits. She brought her special brand of joy on those occasions, helping even the crustiest of parishioners feel better. When the time came to pray, she would take the hand of the person we were visiting, and offer her own, unscripted prayer. I am convinced that those little girl prayers winged their way to God's ears faster than any of mine. Often, I would see a change in those parishioners as peace washed over and through them.

When Alex was ten years old, she came with me to the hospital, where I had been asked to marry a man to his fiancée who was terminally ill with cancer. The nurses had done a wonderful job decorating the room, and the bride wore a wreath of flowers on her bald head. Alex took on the role of wedding photographer, ordering the guests here and there to get the best possible group shots, and generally lifting the mood so much that everyone was in high spirits by the time I performed the ceremony. The bride only lived for two more days, but that wedding was a joyful celebration of life—and it was largely Alex who made it that way.

But our talented, intrepid daughter was hiding serious pain behind her sunny personality. She began to suffer mood swings so severe that they couldn't be blamed on adolescence. We never knew, from one moment to the next, how Alex would react—whether she would scream out her pain and frustration, or withdraw into dark despair. She started to see a therapist, for anxiety and depression.

When Alex was 18 years old, a consulting psychiatrist gave the devastating diagnosis of Borderline Personality Disorder. Our beloved daughter would have to spend the rest of her life learning to control the moods and impulses caused by this incurable condition, while Michael and I tried not to allow ourselves to be hurt when those impulses made her turn on us. Still, the first time she screamed "I hate you!" I could almost hear my heart break.

Alex herself took the fact of her distressing condition surprisingly well. She almost appeared to be proud of the label, although that may have been because she was relieved to have an explanation for the inner turmoil she dealt with every day.

Alex had been living with her boyfriend and his family for five months when she announced that she was pregnant. She was 20 years old by then, and her boyfriend was 19. Michael and I were distraught. But when baby Lily was born, our hearts melted the moment we held her.

That wonderful moment took place in Alex's hospital room on the day of Lily's birth. However, over the next two years, we could count on one hand the number of times we saw our granddaughter in person. This was decreed by Devvin's mother, who apparently believed that adoptive parents have no claim on their adopted child's offspring because they are not blood relatives. For the most part, Alex, whose mental illness made her highly suggestible, abided by that edict. She did sneak in a couple of visits with Michael and me, and she was frequently on the other end of a phone call or video chat.

She was on the phone that morning, my second full day home, with her bubbly voice and her hilarious accounts of little Lily's shenanigans. She is a wonderful mom.

As we used to tell her when she was little, Michael and I love Alex "up to the sky and back again; down to the bottom of the ocean and back again; all around the world and back again." We were not going to say or do anything that might jeopardize the little we saw of her and Lily, and we lived in hope of more.

After my delightful, early morning phone chat with our daughter, the day progressed quietly. I took my pharmacopeia of pills; I drank my strong, dark coffee; I made myself eat some oatmeal, and, later, some soup; and I spent many hours in my glider, reading and writing.

It was a happy, peaceful day. The sun was out, the sky was blue, so I also spent some time sitting in the back yard, wearing SP40, and a wide-brimmed hat so as not to get a sunburned scalp.

Chapter Thirty-two: T-Day Plus Sixteen
One Step Forward

On this momentous day, I had my first neighborhood perambulation!

It was another beautiful day—70 degrees, sunny, and with a refreshing breeze: my favorite kind of weather, and perfect conditions for a walk. But I was concerned that, when we were some distance from home, I might be too tired to walk anymore, and how would we get me home again? Michael was hardly going to carry me! But we still had the wheelchair we'd borrowed when I broke my back, and we came up with an ingenious solution.

We started off with Michael holding Ernie's leash, while I pushed the wheelchair like a walker. Then, after two blocks, when I got tired, I sat in the wheelchair, holding Ernie's leash, while Michael pushed me, and Ernie walked beside me. Our destination was the home of two friends, Jack and Amy, who had just returned from a trip to England, and who lived around four blocks away.

After we'd visited for a while in Amy's beautiful rose garden—at a distance, and with me wearing my mask—I got up to push the wheelchair again while Michael held Ernie's leash. Once again, I managed around two blocks, then we paused and I got back in the wheelchair. So did Ernie! He jumped into my lap and rode the rest of the way home looking extremely pleased with himself.

I was extremely pleased with myself too, having come up with a means of getting some all-important exercise, while not pushing myself so hard that I caused a setback to my recovery. I was, however, so exhausted by our outing, that I fell asleep the moment I sat in my glider and put my feet up. I slept for most of the afternoon, and so did Ernie.

While I was napping, the group texts were flying, thick and fast. There was an in-depth discussion on webbing-style lawn chairs that have become frayed and prone to tearing. Should Lorrie and Robyn buy new chairs, or should they purchase replacement webbing and repair them. "Reduce, reuse, recycle" is a great philosophy to live by, in a world that is being overrun by disposables—but re-weaving lawn chair webbing is time-consuming. And the older the chair, the harder it is to get those screws out...

Paula had been busy sharing old photos from our college years. No digital cameras back then, so she was taking photos of photos in her album, and attaching them to texts. What babies we all were; and of course, we thought we were so grown up. In true feminist form, we insisted on being identified as women from the age of 18.

Now I wish we had allowed ourselves to be girls for just a little longer.

Chapter Thirty-three: T-Day Plus Seventeen
Two Steps Back

One of the many instructions in my post-transplant binder—which was full of them—had to do with fevers. If my temperature exceeded 100.4, I was to call oncology immediately.

I woke up that Sunday morning feeling decidedly punk—shivery, achy, and hot. I don't get fevers very often, but I know when I have one. Sure enough, the thermometer read 100.8. I called oncology. The on-duty doctor sent me to the ER.

The Emergency Room is among my least favorite places on earth. Generally filled with people who are coughing—even if they came in with an injury, they still cough—it's an advertisement for contagion. I am convinced that, if you aren't sick when you arrive in the ER, you will be when you leave.

So, the idea of entering that germ-filled atmosphere, even wearing a mask, filled me with dread. Especially since I was already, apparently, fighting an infection. But the oncologist told me to go, so I did. And as soon as the receptionist heard I was recovering from a stem cell transplant, someone whisked me into a treatment room, safe from the ambient germ population. I should have known there would be nurse angels in the ER too.

If I were just an average Joe (or Joanne) with a temperature of 100.8, I would have a fever. However, because I was a post-stem-cell-transplant Jo with a temperature of 100.8, I had a "Neutropenic Fever" which is a fever accompanied by an abnormally low white blood cell count. I would have to be admitted and given IV antibiotics (the broad-spectrum variety again) until my blood cultures produced some indication of what was wrong. That would be in no fewer than 72 hours. Less than a week after being discharged from the hospital, I was going back in again for a minimum of three days. At least I didn't have to go to Boston this time.

There was a shortage of pillows in my local hospital. This was a real problem, especially in the emergency department, where it had become somewhat of a pillow crisis. I have what my mother used to call a "dowager's hump," which is an upper spinal hunchback that causes one's head to jut forward. It means that, if I lie on my back without a pillow, my head is thrown backwards, my neck is extended, and I am very uncomfortable. That's what was happening when I tried to lie back on my (pillow-less) stretcher in the ER.

But my team of angels wasn't going to allow that situation to carry on. Before long they smuggled a pillow into my cubicle, and I was able to relax.

Soon a nurse came in and accessed the port that was still in place on the right side of my chest. A new set of dingle-dangles was attached, and I started receiving fluids and antibiotics while I was still in the ER, awaiting a bed. As the hours dragged by, a nurse gave me a room service menu and encouraged me to order some dinner, since lunchtime was long gone.

I have learned that, when eating in a restaurant, the most effective method of speeding up the arrival of one's food is to get up and go to the rest room. Invariably, on one's return, the food has materialized. Acting on a similar principle, I placed my dinner order. Sure enough, just a few minutes after I had put down the phone, the wheelchair arrived to take me to my room.

With Michael bringing up the rear, the attendant wheeled me to a medical ward—unlike the transplant ward I'd been on in Boston. The first thing I noticed was that there were two beds in my room. I was already on the verge of a meltdown, just because of being admitted to the hospital; the possibility of having a roommate nearly pushed me over the edge.

"I can't share a room," I whispered to Michael, so urgently that the woman pushing my wheelchair heard me and went off to the nurses' station to tell on me. But that turned out not to be a bad thing, because, when my nurse came in to take my vitals, the first thing she did was to assure me that no one would be occupying the second bed. That was a huge relief, but I was still feeling uncomfortable, especially because the hospital had recently dropped its mask mandate. People, including doctors and nurses, kept coming into my room without wearing them. Whenever someone entered, maskless, I would put my own mask on, and ask them to do the same. Yet the staff never seemed to grasp how vital it was to keep me safe from airborne germs.

I was receiving both fluids and medicine through my port, which meant there were frequent baggie changes. At BWH, that would entail a careful scrub, with an alcohol wipe, of the "hub," which was the part of the IV arrangement that the input lines were attached to. When the hub was no longer in use, it would be covered with a new cap, a supply of which hung on the IV stand for easy access.

None of this was happening in my hometown hospital. The first time I saw a nurse remove a cap, place it face-down on a non-sterile surface, then replace it without so much as a wink at an alcohol wipe, I was horrified. I could practically feel the bacteria entering my body.

It was bad enough being in the hospital but I was also scared. When you are as immunocompromised as I was, being afraid for your health means being afraid for your life. I knew I would be in there for at least three days, and I was already desperate to go home.

Of all things, it was Google that lifted my spirits by sending me a video memory from a few Christmases back. I had recorded an introduction to a seasonal meditation for church, and was delivering it in a suitably reverent fashion. I was practically at the end when, instead of saying "meditation," I said "medication." An inspirational Christmas *medication*. That, of course, made me crack up on camera, and the sight and sound of myself in fits of laughter on the screen of my phone triggered waves of belly laughs, which were just what I needed to counteract my uncomfortable situation. Then Michael returned in time to share my dinner, after the food service managed to track me down.

My world began to shift back into focus.

All the same, I was glad when night fell, because it meant I could cross off a day. With any luck, I would only be there for two more of them.

Chapter Thirty-four: T-Day Plus Eighteen
Now and Then

The high point of this day was when a nurse asked me if I had been a dancer. My room was warm and I was lying on top of the bedsheets, displaying what he declared were "dancer's legs." Since he was the nurse who'd been so cavalier about my IV hubs, he might have been complimenting me to get on my good side—because I had complained about his carelessness to another nurse. Still, I had a look after he'd left the room and decided that my legs really weren't bad for an old lady.

When very bored, one way to pass the time is to turn on the TV and listen for statements that couldn't possibly apply to oneself, and then to say, "Nope. Never going to say that." I was back to watching my comfort food channel, and found myself musing over this comment made by a contestant: "I'm really happy with the grill marks on my plums," she said.

I am certain I will never say, "I'm really happy with the grill marks on my plums." Unless I'm telling this story, of course.

I suppose there are countless things I will probably never say, but it's fun to muse over. And it's better than something the comedian, George Carlin used to do. He would turn on an old movie, and, if there were elderly actors in it, he would say, "That guy is dead now. So's that one. Yup, she's dead."

I enjoy the occasional mishap on TV shows, too. My all-time favorite is the House Hunters episode, featuring a husband and his particularly obnoxious wife seeking their ideal home. She is listing her "must-haves," and describes her final item as "absolutely essential." She specifies "a room that's just for me, where I can go to *decompose*." I'm convinced that the editors left the woman's malapropism in the final broadcast because nobody liked her.

Along with my fascination for daytime television, my hospital routine was starting to look more like my stay at BWH. A sign had finally been placed on my door requiring masks for entry, so I was able to relax. I still put my own mask on though, whenever someone came into the room, so I could be extra safe. I was also having the early morning blood draw that had been such an "entertaining feature" of my previous hospitalization.

On day two of my stay, my blood work indicated that I needed a transfusion. Once again, I had multiple baggies hanging on my IV stand—which remained unnamed because there can only be one Bernie. Mine was probably rolling gently across the floor of some hapless transplant patient in Boston.

My temperature had gone down practically the moment I was admitted, and it remained in the vicinity of normal every time my vital signs were measured. Frankly, I was beginning to feel a bit fraudulent. Yet my oncology team assured me that I was where I needed to be while the cause of my fever spike was being investigated. The hospitalist, too, was adamant that I was not in a fit state to be discharged. He was the one who had ordered my blood transfusion.

So, I stayed where I was and watched Chef Bobby Flay.

When I was in grade school, I stayed home "sick" much more than I had any right to—and there were certainly occasions when I held the thermometer to a light bulb in order to hoodwink my mother. Since I usually had no other symptoms, I'm sure she wasn't fooled, but forcing me to go to school probably wasn't worth the effort. I was nothing if not obstinate. So, home I stayed, eating ice cream, making accessories for the troll village, and doing as little homework as possible. It's amazing I made it through eighth grade.

I thought about those days of truancy, as I sat in my hospital room, waiting to hear the magic word: "discharged." And I mused over how we change as we age, in my case, from a stubborn 12-year-old who took every opportunity to stay home from school, to a stubborn 66-year-old who wanted nothing more than to engage with life, with its full range of responsibilities. There's no doubt about it: cancer compels one to focus on priorities—and to value even the tougher aspects of our existence, because they are all part of being alive.

I had missed the bi-weekly Zoom with my college gang, because I was busy being assessed in the emergency department. My friends made up for it the next day, with texts flying thick and fast, including dozens of photos from Ashley, who is a professional photographer. The heat became the common topic, no matter where the texts originated. From Christine in France, to Robyn in Connecticut, everyone was sweltering—or, like me, relishing their air conditioning. The worst heat and humidity were in Missouri, where poor Lorrie was contending with a broken AC condenser. Her "Comfort Advisor," a fancy name for a salesman, made a temporary fix and advised her that the replacement would take two weeks. We all hoped she would manage to stay cool until then.

Robyn's contribution to the conversation that day was to wonder what our texts would look like if we were Millennials or Gen-Zs. In a long, unpunctuated sentence, all in lower case, and with numerous one- or two-letter abbreviations, she speculated that our communications would look exactly that way. We all agreed that we are happy to be Boomers who text in full, punctuated sentences. We are also card-carrying members of the grammar police, which is frequently the cause of painful frustration.

It's a great feeling to have friends of the same vintage, and to get texts that make sense.

I will never say "lmk f u wan2tlk 2n8"

Chapter Thirty-five: T-Day Plus Nineteen
All-Age Laughter

Michael came to see me three times on this otherwise empty day. Unlike my room at BWH, I had no "Kate's Kitchen" equipped with coffee maker and kettle, so Michael arrived, bright and early, with a cup of French roast. He's a keeper.

Then, because he knew I was bored and fed up, Michael came back during his lunch hour, and ate the sandwich I had ordered for him. His third visit was at the end of the day, when we settled down to watch *Wheel of Fortune* and *Jeopardy* together.

Michael is a software engineer and systems analyst, and can appear to be quite serious and cerebral, but he is actually very goofy. Goofiness is a quality I appreciate in this society that can take itself far too seriously. And there's a place for goofiness at church, too.

Michael's and my favorite comic turn at St. Cat's, was a regular feature of the all-age service, which took place on the first Sunday of the month. The sermon at that service was a children's talk, and often the preachers were a pair of puppets: a sheep named Robert, voiced by Michael, and a pig named Paco, voiced by me.

Robert: Paco, you love Jesus, don't you?

Paco: Of course I love Jesus, Robert, you know I do.

Robert: In that case, do you think you could buy me a double-scoop cone at Ellie's place?

Paco: What does buying you ice cream have to do with loving Jesus?

Robert: Well, that's what Jesus said to Peter, remember? First he asked Peter if he loved him, and, when Peter said he did, Jesus told him to feed his sheep. In fact he told him twice, if you include feeding the lambs... So are we going to Ellie's or not? I'm starving!

Paco: No, we are NOT going to Ellie's! That's not what Jesus meant!

Robert: Well, how about Five Guys then? I could murder a cheeseburger with...

Paco: Don't say it! Don't say it! I'm warning you, Robert!

Robert: Don't say what? All I want is a cheeseburger with...

Paco: NO! Don't say bacon!

Robert: ...fries. Could you buy me a cheeseburger with fries, Paco?

Paco: I will NOT buy you a cheeseburger with fries. And I will NOT buy you ice cream! That's not what Jesus was talking about when he said, "Feed my sheep!"

Robert: Not even a Twinkie? Or a Pop-Tart?

Paco: No, Robert. Jesus didn't mean we should literally feed anyone who happens to look like a sheep.

Robert: I beg your pardon, Paco; I look like a sheep because I am a sheep. And Jesus said you're supposed to feed me.

And so it continued, until a lesson was taught about the gospel reading for the day.

I would be hiding in the pulpit, manipulating both puppets, while voicing Paco. Michael would be in the sound control room with a remote microphone, voicing Robert. It was surprising how many people thought we were both crammed inside the pulpit!

The children loved the puppets, as did most of the adults, who got as much out of the show as the children did—even more, because some of the jokes went over the children's heads.

One couple left the church, however, because of Paco and Robert. It wasn't only the puppets they objected to; it was the mere presence of children in worship services. Rev. Peggy had made little cards for the pews, reminding congregants that "God put the wiggle into children," and that it was important to make them, and their parents, feel welcome, even if they were fidgety or noisy.

The crabby couple was positively insulted by those cards, and by any other suggestion that we delight in the company of little ones as we praise the God who made us all. Frankly we were better off without anti-children parishioners like them.

All-age worship featured monthly at seminary too, where many of the married students had young children. One memorable talk was given by Rev. Daniel, the Dean of Students, a gifted preacher and storyteller, who was an ardent supporter of children in worship. His services featured lots of very small members of the congregation, some lively tunes, much clapping, and big hugs when the time came to "pass the peace"—a special exchange of greetings that takes place among the clergy and congregants, before the celebration of Communion.

On this occasion, Daniel used two chairs for his talk, to illustrate the various ways in which we interact with Jesus throughout our lives: side by side, turned towards him, or turned away from him. After demonstrating a few permutations, Daniel asked for volunteers to suggest some additional positions. The first person who came up spoiled the climax of the talk by putting one chair on the other and explaining that sometimes we need to be held and supported by Jesus. That was exactly what Daniel had been planning to say as a finale.

The next volunteer, one of the students, put both chairs on their sides on the floor, explaining that we sometimes need a snooze. "And our Lord snoozes too?" asked the slightly frazzled Daniel. When the next volunteer took off across the hall, pushing the non-Jesus chair ahead of him—illustrating how sometimes we take great strides forward in our faith—Daniel and the Jesus chair could barely keep up. Further contributions were discouraged at that point.

At the end of the service, we sang a few rousing choruses of I'm Bananas for the Lord (a favorite of the children). Later that afternoon, Suzanne, a student from Sweden, came up to me, looking confused, and asked, "Why were we singing 'I'm a banana' in Communion?"

Another memorable all-age service was the Nativity Play, just before Christmas break. The children, aged between nine months and three years, played the parts of shepherds, sheep, angels, and kings, and so did the grown-ups—all of them. If you had come to the play, you were in the play. I was given a tinsel halo and invited to join the angel contingent, whose job it was to lead the carol-singing.

Mary and Joseph were adults. Jesus was a baby girl with pigtails who sat quite cheerfully in the manger, watching the activity going on around her. I did notice one painfully funny aside while the shepherds were readying themselves for the angels' appearance. Mary said, "Oh, I suppose I should be having a baby now," and proceeded to administer pretend gas and air to herself.

One of the younger kings unwrapped the present she was supposed to give to Jesus, and cried when she found an empty box; some of the small shepherds began beating one another with their sheep; and most of the actors, including me, forgot the words to the carols. We had been instructed to make the appropriate sound effects whenever an animal was mentioned, so, at regular intervals, the room erupted with brays, baas, oinks, and grunts. Not quite a typical nativity play, but close.

Much as he would have liked to, Michael couldn't offer the kind of entertainment we'd both enjoyed through countless all-age services, and the hilarity provided by Robert and Paco, but his very presence—just being there in my hospital room—was a tonic.

My goofy husband makes me laugh, and I make him laugh. That's a requirement that should be part of the marriage vows.

Chapter Thirty-six: T-Day Plus Twenty
Wildlife

At the crack of dawn, I was awakened by my friendly, neighborhood phlebotomist, arriving to collect my blood again for testing. I couldn't get back to sleep after she left, but luckily the Food Network broadcasts 24/7.

Unluckily, my blood work didn't pass muster, and my temperature spiked again. This had been the day I was hoping to go home! That possibility was now off the table. I did leave my room, however, because I was finally moved to a cancer ward, where the staff were more used to patients like me.

Before I was moved, a clergy colleague visited me and talked my ear off for over an hour. I love my friends, but I was utterly exhausted by the time she left. I'd discovered that it wasn't only physical activity that tired me out those days; social activity had a similar effect. The effort of paying attention to someone, and contributing sensibly to a conversation, wore me out.

While I never used to nap, I was getting more than 12 hours of sleep, night and day, on a regular basis. That was not such a bad thing as far as my recovery was concerned, of course; those little cells were still hard at work, multiplying and spreading, even while I was snoozing. Perhaps especially while I was snoozing.

But long visits with non-stop conversation really took it out of me, and I needed to do something about it— without hurting anyone's feelings. My solution was to ask Michael to print a sign for my door, limiting visits to 15 minutes. The very moment he put it up, the wheelchair arrived to take me to my new room, so he took it down again then stuck it on my new door. The next time we looked, it was gone. Apparently only official hospital signs are permitted outside patients' rooms.

On the subject of hospital signs, I was in a hospital in England when a phlebotomist came into my room and told me she'd just seen a cone in the middle of the floor. She looked bemused because "It had a sign on it," she explained, "that said, 'Caution, cone in middle of floor.'"

Changing rooms was the full extent of the day's excitement. My new accommodations were a step up, because there was a shower, but that was the only significant difference. The window view again looked out on the parking lot, but the television was showing nature scenes and playing soothing music. I could almost believe I was in a meadow full of wildflowers. Almost but not quite. I changed the station to the Food Network and made myself comfortable in the recliner.

On this last day of May, I had been indoors for almost the entire month. Blossoms had come and gone, baby birds had fledged, and comfortable temperatures had been replaced by unbearable heat, humidity, and thunderstorms.

Between hospital stays, however, I'd been home long enough to witness an amusing backyard event.

After bears were well and truly out of hibernation, so no longer a threat to our bird feeders, we had put a block of suet in the hanging cage. The next day, the suet was gone, and the cage was latched shut. The thief had been extremely dexterous. A raccoon maybe? We ruled out bears. Yes, a bear had ravaged our suet feeders on previous occasions, but bears rip the cages apart; they don't carefully close and latch them.

Later that day, I happened to glance at a tree with a large hollow in its trunk. There was our block of suet, and there was a happy squirrel thief enjoying his feast. I think he ate the whole thing—which must have had some uncomfortable side effects!

Michael and I are animal lovers. We dote on our pets, and we enjoy watching the wildlife in our backyard, even the suet-robbing squirrels. On a much grander scale we had the experience of a lifetime, observing wildlife on a photo safari in South Africa.

The reserve where we stayed was small by African standards, but it had a fascinating—and photogenic —animal population. At 6:30 every morning and evening, we went out in the jeep with our ranger guide, Bernice. She communicated, by walkie-talkie, with other rangers, so she knew where to take us to have the best possible encounters with rhinos, giraffes, cheetahs, elephants, wildebeest, African buffalo, zebra, lions, and a huge variety of antelopes and birds.

On one of our outings, our jeep was crossing a ravine on a single-track dam. Another jeep, driven by a ranger named James, followed right behind us. All of a sudden, three elephants appeared at the end of the dam, and started walking towards us. Two of them veered off and clambered down the side of the track to a small lake. The remaining elephant continued heading in our direction, and there was no room for him to get past us. Suddenly he extended his ears—a sign of aggression—and broke into a run, coming straight for us. We couldn't back up because of the jeep behind us, and James and his passengers seemed oblivious to the danger we were in.

As the charging elephant got closer and closer, Bernice started screaming into her walkie-talkie, "JAMES! GO JAMES! GO JAMES!" James finally got the message and both jeeps reversed at high speed along the narrow track. When we reached level ground, the elephant ambled past us and nonchalantly joined his two buddies. Apparently, he'd been trying to reach them and we were in the way.

I got it all on video—including Michael saying, when the danger was past, "It's okay now," as though he had personally saved the day.

Another memorable excursion took us to a ridge, overlooking a plain where a large herd of antelope was grazing. We saw a beautiful cheetah seated on the bough of a tree, staring fixedly at the smorgasbord below. So intent was it on eyeing its potential prey, it ignored the jeep full of amateur photographers, allowing us to get near enough for close-up shots. We all turned professional that day, if only for half an hour.

On what would have been Muth's 89th birthday, Michael and I renewed our marriage vows on a bridge, lit by an African sunset. Muth had always dreamed of going to Africa and seeing the wild animals she loved up close. She never managed it, but we did it for her.

Back in the Western hemisphere now, I was hurting. My doctors had decided to make full use of my time in the hospital to re-start the injections that would build up my bone marrow. My every bone, every joint, now played its part in a symphony of pain. Adding insult to injury, daily injections of the anti-coagulant heparin into my belly soon covered it in bruises. I cut my finger shortly after I got home, and the combination of blood thinner and low platelets caused me to bleed, and bleed, like a stuck pig.

I missed my wacky team of BWH nurses, but I was receiving the best possible care from this new batch. I believe that what makes cancer nurses so special is their deep understanding of the illness. Empathy can't be faked; they know what their patients are going through, and they respond to the slightest need—even when it hasn't been put into words. As I got to know my nurses better, I learned that many of them had gone through cancer with a loved one—or had even had it themselves and were survivors. Cancer is ubiquitous and it doesn't play favorites. If you are a human being, you have a one in four chance of a cancer diagnosis, and not everyone survives.

Like the cheetah on the ridge, those murderous cells bide their time and will spring when their prey least expects it. Nobody expects cancer; we anticipate a long, healthy life, with minimal bumps in the road and even fewer detours. But if cancer does attack, we have an abundance of medical professionals on our team, treating us, listening to us, caring for us, and doing their utmost to save our lives. My new nurses were members of that team.

I will go on many more life-changing trips in the years to come. Snorkeling over the Great Barrier Reef is on my bucket list, and so are the Galapagos Islands.

I'm not done yet, and I will never forget the people who made sure of that.

T-Day plus twenty began with me feeling sorry for myself. It ended with me feeling deeply grateful for the life I have already lived, and the life that awaits me—just around the corner.

Chapter Thirty-seven: T-Day Plus Twenty-one
Fevers—and How to Survive Them

As the morning sun made its way into my room, and a care assistant came in to take my vitals, I could tell, as soon as I opened my eyes, that the news was not going to be good. I was shivery and achy, and, sure enough, I had spiked another fever. Because my blood cultures had not provided any useful information, I was no longer receiving IV antibiotics, and this was a setback I really could have done without. And what a setback. When I got up to use the bathroom, my head spun and every joint in my body screamed with pain.

There have been maybe a handful of times in my life when I felt so ill that I could barely move.

One of them took place in the fall of 2000, after Michael and I had gone to see a special Millennium performance of the Passion Play at Oberammergau, Germany. The Play has been performed every ten years, since 1634, in years ending with a zero—with just a few exceptions: post-war conditions in 1920, WWII, and the outbreak of COVID-19. It's a dramatization of events leading up to, and including, the Crucifixion of Christ, performed and produced by more than 2,000 residents of the village.

Michael and I flew into Munich airport, collected our rental car, and set out for Oberammergau.

It was early evening by this time, and already dark. It was also extremely foggy. For one terrifying stretch we couldn't even see past the hood of the car. Michael had to slow to a crawl, while I opened the passenger door enough to see the white line at the edge of the road and prevent Michael from steering into a ditch.

We finally arrived safely at our hotel and were shown to our room.

There, at the end of the bed, was a baby's crib. I'd been pregnant again when we made our reservation, months earlier, and we had failed to let the proprietor know that I had lost our twins. When I saw the crib, I burst into tears.

Our hosts quickly took it away.

The next day was my birthday, and the day of the performance.

The Play was magnificent—every part, even the most minor extras, played with enormous skill and fervor. There were real animals, realistic effects, accurate costumes, stirring music—every aspect of the production conveyed the tragedy and the glory of events that are central to our faith. It was an experience of a lifetime.

Michael and I stayed in Germany for another week, exploring the beautiful island of Mainau, and meeting up with a friend of Michael's from his college year in Frankfurt. We also enjoyed many delights of German cuisine.

The day before we were due to fly home, I woke up feeling awful, aching all over, and clearly feverish, although we had no thermometer. Michael asked the hotel receptionist to find us a doctor. Soon we were sitting in the examining room of the kind and gentle Herr Doktor Muthmann.

I have already observed how God sometimes uses technology to speak to us. This time God used the screen on the doctor's desktop computer. While he was out of the room and I was slumped on his examining table, a single word scrolled across the monitor: "Muth." It was clearly a screensaver made from a shortened form of the name Muthmann, but it was also what Joanie and I called our mother. Just seeing her name in that foreign place brought me comfort.

We went back to the hotel with a packet of pills, and I went back to bed. But I felt worse and worse as the day wore on. Finally, when I could no longer stand the pain I was in, Michael called Doctor Muthmann again—and, amazingly, he made a house call to our hotel room! This time he gave me an injection. I have no idea what it was, and I'm sure it wouldn't be approved by the AMA, but it worked. The pain went away, I slept through the night, and I woke up the next morning feeling completely well.

We flew home without incident. Although the flu came back again in earnest the next day, I will never forget Herr Doktor Muthmann, his magic shot, and his motherly computer screen.

Now, back in my hospital room two decades later, I felt better as the morning progressed. By lunchtime the fever had gone and I no longer ached in every corner of my body.

I had also received some great news. My college friend, Christine, who'd been living in various parts of Europe for the past thirty years, was visiting the States. She and her husband had recently bought a condo in France, and she had returned to arrange for the shipping of items from storage. She was staying with her sister, less than an hour's drive from the hospital, and she wanted to see me before she flew home.

We agreed on an early morning visit the following day. The prospect of seeing a long-time friend did wonders for my state of health and mind.

Michael arrived in time to share my dinner and watch our game shows. The day had ended in a much better fashion than it began.

The wonderful thing about having a fever is how good you feel when you no longer have one. It's almost like being reborn!

Chapter Thirty-eight: T-Day Plus Twenty-two
Youthful Adventures

Christine wasn't kidding when she said she would arrive early in the morning; it was 7:30 when she knocked on my door. She was dressed in French chic, and brought a gift from her sister, who is a talented quilter. Christine actually brought three quilts so I could choose my favorite, an abstract design of window frames in purples and blues. It's a masterpiece!

The two of us marveled over the fact that my furthest-away friend was the first to manage a visit. She was flying back to France the next day, but we had plenty of time to catch up, in that way good friends have of picking up where we left off months, even years, before.

As I so often do, I thanked God for the people who enrich my life daily. There's nothing quite like friendships that endure for decades.

However, for my third year of college, I deserted my dear friends and flew to England for my junior year abroad. It was a year of adventures, new friendships, academic forays, and the kind of wing-spreading that 21-year-olds do the world over, when they are let loose, far from home!

I had come from a small women's college to a large coed university, and, from day one, I was determined to make the most of it. On the day I arrived, there was a showcase of dozens of committees and clubs that students could join. Much to my father's dismay, I signed up for the Labour party and, much to my mother's delight, I signed up for a Bible study group.

There were two other members of that group, a professor and another student, and we met weekly, in my dorm room, throughout the first semester. Those two men were so patient with me! I knew next to nothing about the Bible at that stage in my life, nor had I any inkling of the vocation I would be called to fifteen years down the line. I asked stupid questions such as, "What did Jesus have against 'the world and the flesh?' I get why he'd be anti-devil, but the world's kind of a nice place, and if we didn't have flesh, we'd just be a bunch of bones." And they would respond with such kindness and forbearance that I ended up with a smattering of biblical knowledge I would draw upon in years to come.

Unfortunately, when the second semester rolled around, I became distracted by the world and the flesh, and gave up meeting with my patient Bible tutors. But I'll never forget them, and I'll always be grateful to them.

One of my adventures that year, 1978, was the two weeks I spent on a kibbutz in Kiryat Gat, Israel during spring break. The kibbutz was located in the middle of acres of orange and grapefruit groves, and had a factory that made electric fans. Most volunteers wanted to harvest fruit; I liked manufacturing the intricate hubs that held the fan blades. Every morning, I would put on my factory worker uniform and take my place in the assembly line. I loved every minute of it, and made friends with several of my Palestinian co-workers.

One evening, two of them took me to the southernmost edge of the kibbutz, which was bordered with razor wire separating it from something like a barren no-man's-land. My friends warned me never to venture beyond the confines of the kibbutz because there was a real danger of being caught up in conflict.

On a couple of occasions, I was assigned kitchen duty—once to clean, and the second time to make matzoh balls for the upcoming Passover holiday. That was my first experience of matzoh balls, and I ate close to a quarter of my output. They didn't even make it as far as the soup. The other kibbutz delicacies were oranges and grapefruits, straight off the trees, that my roommates would bring back from the daily harvests. It was the only time I have peeled and eaten a grapefruit like an orange; they were that juicy and sweet.

I was in Israel on Easter Day that year, and two of my roommates and I hitchhiked to Jerusalem, with the intention of attending a service at the famed Church of the Holy Sepulcher. What we hadn't anticipated was that the place would be mobbed! There are a dozen or more little chapels in the ancient building, each one a different denomination and language, and each one of which was hosting its own separate Easter service.

There were throngs of tourists, several television cameras and news reporters, and nuns, monks, and priests at every turn. It was almost as though they were expecting the Second Coming. My friends and I escaped from the clouds of incense, into the fresh air, and hitchhiked back to the kibbutz.

On my final night in Kiryat Gat, one of my roommates and I decided to sleep out in the open. It was a beautiful, clear, chilly, and starry, starry night. I woke up the next morning with the mother of all head colds.

On my return to the UK, I was due to look after the two young sons of a professor from my home college, while he and his wife took a trip. When they picked me up from the airport, we discovered that I had temporarily gone almost completely deaf from the combination of aircraft pressure and congestion.

I had also lost my sense of smell. After the parents left and the weather grew colder, I switched on the electric blanket on my bed before going to sleep. In the middle of the night, the two boys rushed into my room. "We smell something burning!" they shouted, "Don't you smell it?" I didn't, but it was my bed that was on fire. One corner of the foam rubber mattress was bubbling away—thankfully not the part I was sleeping on. My electric blanket had malfunctioned, and it was fortunate that the boys had working nostrils. I put out the fire and we all went back to bed.

When my professor and his wife came home, I could smell and hear again.

......

Shortly after Christine's early morning visit, my doctors arrived on their daily rounds.

They made their announcement with happy smiles. "The signs are all good, and we're discharging you! Your temperature has stayed down; and your bloodwork showed nothing sinister. There's no reason to keep you."

By mid-afternoon I was home again, with an ecstatic puppy, an insouciant cat, and a grateful husband.

Chapter Thirty-nine: T-Day Plus Twenty-three
Tribulations

It was a good feeling to wake up back home, and to have my husband bring me my morning coffee—which is something he has done almost every day since we were first married. There are several tasks besides coffee in Michael's domain. He's responsible for the garbage and recycling; he does most of the grocery shopping; and he replaces empty toilet paper rolls. He is the computer expert, and he takes care of anything to do with our cars, from registration renewal to services and inspections. He also takes care of Charlie's litter box. He started doing that the first time I was pregnant—because we had been warned that cat poop is dangerous to pregnant women—and he's done it ever since. He's an awfully handy man to have around.

For a number of years, Michael has worked from home, for a company where every employee works remotely. His situation has been a godsend, not only during my transplant recovery but on other occasions when driving was difficult—if not impossible. When I was hampered by my two broken wrists, for example, I never could have gotten myself to work, doctors' appointments, or any other destination, without his help.

When we first moved from the west coast, Michael's job was in another state, nearly a three-hour drive away. He'd been interviewed over the phone during our cross-country drive, a memorable occasion when I left him to his conversation while I got out of the car and read a book, leaning against the passenger door.

Michael got the job and moved to Maine, where he rented a room from a young couple. Alex and I would see him at weekends, but he was gone the rest of the time.

Those three years were a tremendous strain—on our marriage, and on our daughter. With no one at home to care for her, I had to take Alex to every evening meeting, settling her in some corner where she could do her homework or watch a video on her tablet. It was far from an ideal situation, but I couldn't afford to pay a babysitter every time I had an evening obligation. Alex also had to come to church at the end of every school day and was expected to do her homework while her mother did her job. She grew up resenting the institution that had robbed her of parental attention, and I can't say that I blame her.

I became a single parent during the entire working week, and it took its toll—especially as I was grieving my parents at the same time, both of whom died during the time I spent apart from my husband. For his part, Michael was lonely, missing his "girls" and facing empty evenings every weekday. When he arrived home on Friday nights, we both had expectations of a rejuvenating two days together, but weekends were my busiest time at church, so we were almost never able to relax.

When Michael found a position less than an hour's drive from our home, it felt like a gift at first, until he began to experience the job's extremely high pressure. It affected him both emotionally and physically.

Michael kept an eye on the recruitment agencies, and, after nearly four years, he spotted something that was right up his alley. He had a telephone interview one afternoon. After an hour, when I could still hear Michael chatting and laughing, I knew he had the job.

Almost immediately, the mood changed in our household. Michael and I would have stayed together no matter how demanding his job might be, but what a world of difference when his commute changed from an hour on the freeway to a trip downstairs. Although he could, he has never spent a working day in his pajamas.

Meanwhile Alex was in the throes of adolescence, and nothing we could say or do would convince her that we loved her unconditionally. Alex is an example of a phenomenon known as PK, "Priest's Kid"—a status that led to some very turbulent years.

A parish priest, by definition, is committed to her congregation, readily available to meet pastoral needs of all kinds. Marriages and baptisms are scheduled well in advance, but illness and death can happen at any time. On all too many occasions my daughter's needs took second place to the needs of my parishioners. I feel deep regret that I will never get those years with Alex back again.

Alex was also dealing with the circumstances of her adoption, which had become more of an issue because she had made contact with her birth family in England. In the time-honored fashion of disgruntled teens, Alex reacted by neglecting her schoolwork and spending time with an unscrupulous crowd. She dropped out of high school and was pregnant at twenty.

And then she turned her life around. Alex earned her GED; she got herself a good job, and she's raising her daughter with enormous love and great skill. I am so proud of her.

Michael and I did our best to make up for the demands of parish life by having some wonderful vacations with Alex. We made the move to the States just before she turned three. From there we flew to the Hawaiian islands of Kauai and Maui, made several visits to New England, and had a memorable trip to Finland—where we kept forgetting to go to bed because the sun never set.

For Alex's fourth birthday, we went on a mini cruise to Catalina and Mexico. Michael and I contracted norovirus and spent the entire four days in our cabin, but Alex stayed well and had a great time participating in the ship's excellent children's program.

Whatever bug had landed me in the hospital this time was well and truly gone, and I was starting to feel stronger than I had been since before the transplant. Michael and I took some more walks, accompanied by the wheelchair for when my energy ran out, and Ernie pulled his trick of riding home on my lap. Life was settling into a healthy routine, and I was even beginning to appreciate retirement.

But I still didn't love it.

Chapter Forty: T-Day Plus Twenty-four
Staying Connected

Sunday morning arrived, sunny and fresh, and it was time for church. Because of my compromised immune system, church meant powering up my laptop, attending services virtually, and joining in a special "Prayer for Spiritual Communion" instead of receiving the Eucharist. St. Cat's service was the one Michael and I chose to stream, although it was often painful, seeing people I loved getting up to do the Bible readings and lead the prayers. I missed our parishioners so much. And, of course, it wasn't easy to watch another priest doing my job! But we would sing along with the hymns with gusto and say the familiar prayers without even referring to the Book of Common Prayer. It was nothing like being there in person, but at least we were gettin' religion.

The streaming of Sunday services was a recent feature of worship at St. Cat's. It grew out of adjustments we made during the pandemic, when a "lockdown" was put in place to prevent the very contagious COVID-19 virus from spreading. The last day we gathered in the building was March 15, 2020.

We had already taken other precautions against the virus. The shared cup was no longer in use; Communion consisted of wafers only; and hand sanitizer was dispensed prolifically. We had also requested that congregants not touch one another when passing the Peace. The hugs and hand clasps that were so much a part of St. Cat's warm fellowship were replaced by waves and "Namaste" gestures. And, of course, we had to discontinue the popular coffee hour.

After the 10:00 service that day, we all went home. And stayed home, away from our church building, for more than a year.

When COVID hit, we were nearly halfway through Lent, and three weeks away from Holy Week. How were we going to provide worship opportunities for the most important seasons in the Church year, when we couldn't gather in person? I knew there was only one solution, a technical one. I purchased video software for my laptop and taught myself how to use it in a day. And then I became what they never taught us in seminary: a director/producer/presenter/editor/broadcaster of online worship services.

Every day during lockdown, we offered a service of Morning Prayer, with Bible texts read by parishioners I had recorded over Zoom. Then on Saturday afternoon, there was a live Zoom service. Instead of Communion, participants partook of their own agape meal—a small serving of bread or crackers or cookies, and a glass of wine or juice to sip. It didn't qualify as Eucharist because our bishop believed that consecration, the special blessing of the bread and wine, couldn't happen online—and I agreed with him. But it was a comforting act that brought us together in the symbolic sharing of a meal. Only a few regulars participated but we gathered faithfully and virtually—a close-knit group.

Sunday morning's offering was a compilation of the familiar liturgy, Bible readings and prayers offered by parishioners, and hymns that had been expertly produced by Heather, our talented Director of Music Ministries, and her tech-savvy husband, Larry. Once again, The Prayer for Spiritual Communion was included instead of Eucharist or agape.

Every Friday, the florist we used for altar flowers would deliver two arrangements that I displayed on my dining room sideboard, converted to an altar with a linen cloth, candles, and ribbons in the appropriate liturgical colors. That was my background as I led the prayers, preached, and gave a final blessing.

I suppose I had a double standard: I couldn't accept cyber-consecration, but I was in no doubt that blessings positively flew through the airwaves—and that they traveled in both directions. Whether we were in the same room or not, my congregation was as much a blessing to me as I strived to be to them.

On the first Sunday of the month, we kept up the all-age service tradition with our puppets: The Gospel According to Paco and Robert. We even had a little theme song, composed and performed by Larry, with input from the puppets.

For the Easter service, I had four enormous potted lilies delivered, which I displayed on and around my "altar." I then recorded the service—including an off-the-cuff sermon—with a new, improved video package I was using for the first time. When I had finished, I put two of the lily plants in my car and delivered them to a couple of parishioners who had recently been in the hospital. Back home again, I sat down to edit the Easter service—and discovered, to my horror, that there was no sound!

To this day I don't know what I did wrong, but I had to record the entire service again, including an approximate repetition of the sermon I had delivered previously, sans script. And now only two lilies decorated the altar. I could have taken back the ones I had given away, but that would have been churlish.

Finally, the service was complete, with prelude and hymns, and it was ready to be broadcast on Easter Day. It received 270 views—around five times the usual number for a Sunday service. But then, Easter is no ordinary day.

One of the most remarkable aspects of the lockdown was how quickly folks adapted to online communication. People who'd never even heard of Zoom were using it regularly. That meant we could maintain the human connections, which were so much a part of St. Cat's. One very popular weekly event was our virtual coffee hour. Every Sunday, up to 30 parishioners and I would gather over Zoom, and spend an hour chatting while we sipped our coffee or tea.

Our virtual coffee hour continued even after we were back in the building. Two regulars at that gathering were Matt and Robert, who joined us from their home in Wisconsin. Theirs is a bittersweet story.

On a beautiful fall day in October 2020, I had married Matt to his delightful fiancé, Dan. COVID-19 affected attendance somewhat, but the small group of family and friends clearly adored the couple. I married them outdoors, in a small clearing on the grounds of the inn where they would hold their reception. The foliage was glorious, and there was an autumnal breeze that caught my vestments and made me look as though I were about to take off. But I managed to stay earthbound, and the ceremony went without a hitch. Dan was one of the most joyful people I've ever known and their wedding day reflected that joy.

Less than three months later, I had a phone call from Matt. Dan had suffered a heart attack while shoveling snow. He died instantly, only 60 years old. The two of them had been attending our virtual coffee hour together for months, with Dan's infectious smile brightening up the Zoom screen. They had made many friends in our parish, despite living in the mid-west, and we were all devastated to hear of Dan's untimely death.

But Matt's story wasn't over yet. A year later, he brought a new friend to coffee hour. He and Robert had met through an online dating service, and they were now living together. A few months later they asked me to come to Wisconsin the following October to marry them. It was like a fairy tale—and when I said so to Matt and Robert, they laughed hard at my choice of words.

My biopsy surgery and cancer diagnosis, however, took place just two weeks before I was due to fly to Milwaukee, and I had to send my sad regrets. Another Episcopal priest was able to step in at the last minute, but we were all disappointed that I was unable to share in their special day. Matt and Robert are now in the process of building their dream house together, and they have a blended family of five dogs who rule the roost. They are blissfully happy, and a wonderful testament to love's healing power.

......

At the end of June 2021, St. Cat's parishioners gathered for a service of Holy Eucharist in the parking lot of the church building. It was the first time we had been together, in person, since COVID first reared its ugly head. Most of the congregation had contracted COVID-19 by that time, and some of the cases had been severe, but we hadn't lost anyone to the virus. We were strong and determined, and nothing was going to get us down.

During the many months I had been ministering from home, I had gotten into the habit of wearing comfortable clothing and no shoes. When the world began to open up again, and I was back in my office, I found it very difficult to go back to a clerical collar, especially as July was particularly hot and humid that year.

One day the organist from another parish dropped by St. Cat's to pick our brains on how we were dealing with in-person worship, specifically singing. When I came out of my office to greet him, the first thing he said to me was, "You're not wearing a collar!"

It's a good thing he didn't look down, because I wasn't wearing any shoes, either.

Chapter Forty-one: T-Day Plus Twenty-five
In Good Hands

Nearly four weeks after my transplant, and two weeks after my discharge from BWH, I had what would have been my first consultation with my local oncologist, Dr. Lovato. However, because of my recent sojourn in the hospital, and especially because he had been on call the weekend I was admitted, I had been seen by him, or by a member of his team, for five days in a row. Still, it was important to keep this appointment because it would provide a baseline for future visits to oncology, every two weeks, for bloodwork and check-ups with Dr. Lovato or one of his physician's assistants.

My oncology team was both thorough and cautious— my recent hospitalization being a case in point. A raised temperature for a neutropenic post-transplant patient could turn nasty very quickly, defeating the whole purpose of my cutting-edge treatment. An infection could easily turn to sepsis, for example, which could prove to be fatal if not caught and treated in a timely manner.

The day before the previous Thanksgiving, when I was still receiving my monthly chemotherapy treatments, pre-transplant, I had noticed that the skin around my port looked crusty. It was clear that the site had become infected. I knew I had an appointment scheduled with the oncologist in two days, so I poured hydrogen peroxide on the incision, applied a gauze bandage, and didn't give it another thought.

On Thanksgiving morning, I cleaned and covered the site again, and set about putting the finishing touches on a stuffed pumpkin and a pumpkin cheesecake—our contributions to dinner at our friends', Jack and Amy's, house. We had a wonderful time with them, and arrived home as stuffed as the pumpkin I'd prepared.

The next morning, I went to my appointment with Doctor Lovato, who took one look at my port and got on the phone with the hospital. Within two hours, I was on the table in an operating room, trying to remain conscious through my conscious sedation, while the infected port was removed. Because of the danger of re-infection, the surgeon couldn't suture the wound. Instead, it was packed and dressed, and I was taken to my room to begin receiving IV antibiotics. I was in the hospital for three days before the results of my blood cultures revealed a surface staph infection, and I was allowed to go home.

My infected port crisis had a happy ending, but it could have gone in a completely different direction. Before dispatching me to the OR, Dr. Lovato had read me the riot act for failing to contact his office the moment I first noticed that I had a problem. If it had proven to be an infection in my blood, waiting two days would have been very dangerous, because sepsis progresses rapidly and can be resistant to treatment.

I was chastened by Dr. Lovato's reprimand, but I was secretly glad I had been foolhardy. If I had done the right thing, Michael and I would have missed out on a lovely Thanksgiving celebration with our dear friends, at a time when our social life was already severely curtailed. Sometimes our mental health has to take precedence over our physical health—and, try as I might, I couldn't rustle up much regret. I was, however, very careful to abide by the rules after that incident, which was why my elevated temperature had landed me in the hospital for five days.

At my day-25 check-up, Dr. Lovato pronounced me cured of whatever illness had afflicted me. An infection never showed up in my blood cultures, so he ruled it a virus, and he was happy with the results of that day's bloodwork as well. Slowly but surely, the healthy cells that had been returned to my bloodstream, were multiplying and spreading. My platelets, and my red and white corpuscles, were still far below normal levels, but they were on their way.

My future was looking brighter than ever.

I continued to feel like a fraction of my former self, however. My energy level was unpredictable—at times almost non-existent—and I was still sleeping a lot during the day, which was something I never used to do. But I was improving daily; I could tell. I could take a shower without feeling so exhausted after-wards that I had to go back to bed. I could make my own cup of tea without having to sit down while I waited for it to steep. And I could take progressively longer walks, pushing my trusty wheelchair, before Ernie and I were ready to be trundled home again.

One thing that was still not cooperating was my appetite. I had never in my life had a problem with eating. Let me rephrase that: the only problem I'd ever had was eating too much. Loss of appetite had never been my issue. But after the biopsy of the tumor in my throat, when I couldn't manage anything other than soup for a few weeks, I never got back to normal, even after that wound had healed. In the space of four months, I lost nearly 30 pounds. It was weight I could afford to lose, but it was the wrong way to go about it!

After my stem cell transplant, not only did I generally not feel like eating, but when I did try, food was tasteless, as if I were eating paper. Michael kept trying to tempt me with tasty meals from our freezer, but I would take just a few bites, then give the rest to him. The more weight I lost, the more he gained! My oncology team was aware of the problem. They kept pushing a high calorie, high nutrition drink that comes in a variety of flavors and, in my opinion, tastes awful. I did try, but I found it undrinkable. Most of the time I was relying on my old standby, soup. Dave, our caregiver's caregiver, took over our kitchen one afternoon and cooked up several pots of hearty, delicious concoctions to tempt me. For the most part, it helped, but I had a long way to go before I was back to three squares a day.

I had a long way to go before I had a full head of hair again, too. I was starting to look more like a large, fuzzy peach than an oversized billiard ball, as, slowly, my hair was coming back. It looked as though it would be the same color as before, but it was too early to tell whether curly or straight. A blond, straight-haired friend of mine had chemotherapy which caused her to lose her hair. It grew back gray and curly. My hair was already gray but it had never been naturally curly. My secret hope was that I would produce a halo of curls.

When I worked in London, I found a hairdressing school, where members of the public could have their hair done at reduced prices. I booked myself in for a perm. When the time came, I was assigned two students, one for each side of my head. It wasn't until they had both finished putting the rollers in, that they realized they had been using two different techniques. The two students, as well as their supervisor, seemed very concerned about the error, but I just figured curls are curls. I was wrong. When the rollers were removed and my hair was washed and dried, half of my head looked like a young Shirley Temple, and the other half like Jennifer Grey in *Dirty Dancing*. It took a year for my hair to grow enough to cut off all those ringlets and curls.

Lopsided hairdos notwithstanding, it's important to give learners the opportunity to practice on live humans. After all, my brilliant oncologists were students themselves once upon a time, and now they're saving my life.

It isn't only doctors who work at perfecting their skills. Every appointment I had in oncology, including this day's, began with a visit to the lab to have blood drawn. Every time, the phlebotomist would warn me, "Quick pinch," and, every time, the needle would go in so smoothly and skillfully that I never felt a thing. I think the phlebotomists appreciated having a patient who didn't make a fuss; the truth was, they were remarkably good at their job.

The needle tracks on my arms, however, made me look like an addict.

Chapter Forty-two: T-Day Plus Twenty-six
Breaking Out of Prison

This morning, I was walloped with a severe case of cabin fever—the kind that couldn't be cured by sitting in the back yard or taking a walk in the neighborhood. I wanted out in a big way. I wanted to go on a vacation, or see a movie on a big screen, or just stroll through a shopping mall or a grocery store. I desperately wanted to do normal things, even though my body was far from normal, and my immune system was still puny.

I tried telling myself that I felt that way because I was getting stronger, more like my old self, but that just made me antsier. My old self wasn't a prisoner in my own home, for crying out loud. Oh yes, I had it bad.

It's a widely held misconception that parish ministry is limited to the parish. To some extent it is: presiding at worship services, preaching, leading Bible studies and other spiritual formation, and pastoral counseling—all these take place in the church building. But there is much that happens beyond those four walls. Examples are visits to homebound or hospitalized parishioners, grave-side funeral services, and chaplaincy duties for local organizations.

Ministry can and does happen anywhere, and it is often most effective when it takes place away from home base. It is also healthy for a priest to get out and about, to follow the example set by Jesus in identifying where there are needs and doing one's best to meet them.

One of the features of my seminary training was an inner-city placement, which included a ride-along with a local police officer. The night I took my turn in the patrol car, the officer received a call to respond to a threatened suicide on one of the city's towering bridges. When we arrived at the scene a man was clinging to the girders on the wrong side of the structure. The police officer had already explained to me that if the man were to hit the water flat on, it would be like hitting concrete. If he entered the water vertically, he would likely get stuck in the mud and drown. Either way, jumping from that height would almost certainly prove fatal.

The officer approached the man slowly, and gently asked him what the trouble was. The man said that his girlfriend had broken up with him and he didn't want to live anymore. But he stayed where he was, holding tightly to the girders. After around five minutes of reassuring the man and reminding him of how many people would be affected if he died, the officer said, "There's a lady vicar here; why don't you talk to her?"

I was terrified. What if he didn't approve of the ordination of women? What if I reminded him of his girlfriend and he took one look at me and jumped?

Following the officer's example, I moved a few steps closer, and spoke carefully of God's love and comfort. Thankfully, the man stayed put and listened. Together, the officer and I did our best to convince the man that he was a precious child of God as well as a valued member of his family and circle of friends. And finally, he made the heart-stopping climb back to safety. We drove him to the police station. From there, he called his sister, who arrived in tears of relief and took him home.

I believe that God's work was done on that bridge— as much by the police officer as by a terrified seminarian, temporarily promoted to "lady vicar."

A year or so into my curacy, I had a hospital appointment for an endoscopy. This was the UK's National Health Service, so it was definitely a no-frills procedure. After I was done, I was wheeled out to a recovery area where there were half a dozen other stretchers lined up, side by side. As I was lying there, a doctor came out to speak to the man on the stretcher next to me, about the results of his endoscopy. There, in front of us all, the doctor told the man that he had an inoperable malignant mass. I was appalled. The poor man had received a death sentence, publicly. With both of us recovering from the effects of the anesthesia, all I could think to do was to take the man's hand and pray for his peace of mind.

I found out, weeks later, that the man I had tried to console at the hospital that day was the husband of a member of my congregation. I was able to accompany him throughout his cancer journey, to preside at his funeral when the end came, and to provide comfort to his widow.

Offering prayers and blessings, in a variety of settings and circumstances, has always been a significant— and cherished—part of my ministry.

One of my favorite celebrations is the annual Blessing of the Animals—on or around the feast of St. Francis (October 4). All of my parishes have hosted services to which pets are invited, and I have blessed everything from a goat to a walking stick insect. In addition to the services in the building, I've often taken the blessings to the great outdoors, setting up a sign in the town center, donning vestments, and accosting any passerby with a canine companion. Many of these dog owners tell me they have no religious affiliation, but nothing is too good for their beloved pups. My simple prayers—for good health and long life, gratitude for loyal companionship, bright eyes, lively energy, whatever comes to mind as I gaze into those doggie faces—are welcomed and appreciated. Perhaps even by the dogs.

It's my conviction that the blessing of pets encourages their owners' belief that a God who cares about animals is a God worth getting to know better.

As my cabin fever raged, I did my best to distract myself from what felt like imprisonment by reminiscing over my past forays into church beyond the building. Not one of them required the presence of a priest—or even a priest in training. The police officer, who enlisted my help with a man poised to take his own life, was a prime example of a layperson living out the gospel, whether he was a believer or not. There are similar opportunities presenting themselves all the time—although, thankfully, not necessarily on the scale of a suicide bid.

Whether it's taking the time to celebrate the bond between human and animal, or to speak kindly to someone in pain, or to comfort someone who is bereaved—or even facing their own death—we are invited to go where need exists, and to do what we can to meet that need. Every human being is called to be a minister, and each one of us is equipped to make a difference in the lives of others.

I could talk to fellow patients in the waiting room, as we awaited our oncology appointments. There were receptionists, phlebotomists, nurses, and doctors, too, and my encounters with every one of them gave me a chance to channel God's love—even if all I did was smile and listen. At home, there were phone conversations, Zoom gatherings, texts, and emails—there were so many opportunities to share affection, joy, encouragement, and other signs of God's grace.

I couldn't go on vacation. I couldn't even go to a grocery store. But I was alive and able, and I was willing to do whatever I could within the confines of my shrunken world. And, like my hair, my world was already beginning to grow again.

Chapter Forty-three: T-Day Plus Twenty-seven
Name Dropping

The day began with a call from one of the oncology physician's assistants, with the test results on a stool sample I had provided the day before. "We know why you've been feeling so rotten," she said. "You have C-Diff."

Clostridioides difficile is a bacterial infection of the colon, which can cause diarrhea, abdominal pain, loss of appetite, nausea, and fever. Or, in my case, all of the above. It can result from a heavy dose of antibiotics, which kill good bacteria along with the bad, but it is highly infectious, and older adults with compromised immune systems, like yours truly, are particularly susceptible. It's likely that I picked it up during one of my hospital stays—an irony which did not pass my notice.

When the PA gave me the news, I blurted out, "Oh shit!"

"Exactly," was her reply.

I was prescribed a powerful antibiotic, which seemed like a contradiction since antibiotics can cause the infection, but I was told to take an equally powerful probiotic to counter the side effects. C-Diff is notoriously hard to get rid of—which may be why it's called "difficile," but I was optimistic. I had been suffering from the symptoms for so long, without knowing what was causing them, and the possibility of a cure raised my spirits enormously. Maybe I would even get my appetite back, although I did not want to gain back the weight I had lost over the past year; my newly svelte figure was the one silver lining of my condition.

I have only been svelte, for a few months at a time, on a handful of occasions in my life. Overweight from the age of eight, dieting has always been one of my least favorite activities. Exercise is another. But once in a while I would rustle up some self-discipline and get down to an acceptable number on the scale—which I would celebrate by purchasing thin-girl clothes. One such outfit, back in the early eighties, was a pair of black satin pants, black suede knee-high boots, and a silky, white oversized shirt. I wore this ensemble on a first date with a man I had been eyeing for months. Tall, smart, and personable, Lewis was my kind of guy, and I really wanted to make a good impression on him.

Lewis took me to a friend's party, and everything was going swimmingly, until a buffet dinner was laid out and people perched wherever they could find a spot to eat their meal. I had gone upstairs for a moment, and when I was about to go back down, the heel came off one of my boots. I started to lose my balance. I put the other foot down to save myself, and the heel came off that boot too, landing me on my backside at the top of the stairs.

Unfortunately, my satin pants were very slippery. I instantly started sliding down, at top speed, scattering the half dozen guests who had chosen to sit on the steps to eat their dinner. When I reached the bottom, there was my date, looking both horrified and embarrassed. In my wake, there were several irritated diners, picking up sausage rolls, disemboweled sandwiches, and other food detritus knocked off their plates during my torpedo-like descent. We left the party shortly afterwards—with me struggling to stay upright in my heelless boots—and Lewis dropped me off at my apartment. There was no goodnight kiss. And no second date.

In another one of my svelte periods, I donned a size eight gown with enormous shoulders—in the eighties, of course—for a fundraiser ball held by my employers. None other than Prince Philip was one of the esteemed guests, and he and his cohort were the objects of many sideways glances. But this was England; one simply did not intrude upon the privacy of the Queen's consort—not even with something as innocuous as a "How d'you do, your Royal Highness?"

At 2:00 AM, a sumptuous breakfast was laid out on tables by the side of the dance floor, and I went up to fill my plate—after all, it had been more than two hours since supper. As I was helping myself to the kedgeree (a traditional Indian dish of fish and rice), I heard a voice over my left shoulder.

"D'you think they would bring us some forks?"

It was Prince Philip.

"I think they would if you asked them," I replied. I was so flustered that I forgot to say "your Royal Highness," but he didn't seem to mind.

He got his fork.

Not all of my elbow rubbing was with royalty. Several memorable encounters took place with actors. One such occasion occurred around ten years after the kedgeree incident, when Michael had written a Pentecost Sunday skit to be performed for our parish. The skit was inspired by Jesus' disciples' sudden ability to speak in foreign languages, and was based on a Star Trek episode that featured the Universal Translator—a futuristic gadget that converted any language into English, allowing the Starship crew to communicate with alien beings.

It so happened that Michael and I had tickets to a play at the local theatre the night before Pentecost Sunday, and starring in the play was Patrick Stewart, the actor who played Captain Jean-Luc Picard in *Star Trek: The Next Generation*.

Although it was Captain Kirk who commanded the Enterprise in Michael's Universal Translator episode, that didn't stop me from writing to Mr. Stewart, care of his agent, inviting him to attend our Pentecost service and play the part of Captain Kirk in the skit. A few days later, Michael and I came home to find a message from Patrick Stewart on our answering machine. He thanked us for thinking of him, but sent regrets that he was unable to take the part because he had to leave town right after his Saturday evening performance.

The story didn't end there. Michael and I attended Mr. Stewart's play, as planned, and went to the stage door afterwards to give our good wishes to the great man. In front of us a quartet of teenaged youths joked around and jostled each other as they waited for their TV hero to emerge. Several other people arrived to queue up behind us, autograph books and programs at the ready.

Then the stage door opened, and Patrick Stewart came out. The rowdy teens were instantly struck dumb, unable even to respond when Mr. Stewart greeted them. He left them gaping and came down the steps to where Michael and I were standing.

"Hello, Mr. Stewart," I said, reaching out to shake his hand. "I'm Kate Atkinson. Thank you so much for your phone call. And this is Michael, the playwright."

As we were warmly welcomed by Captain Picard, the rest of the fans withdrew slightly, with an awed intake of breath. Clearly, we were important people who traveled in august circles. Except, of course, we weren't, really.

Michael ended up playing the part of Captain Kirk the next day, but our encounter with the kind and genuine Patrick Stewart buoyed us up for a long time to come.

My sister Joanie and I had waited outside that same stage door some years earlier, after attending a production of *The Admirable Crichton* featuring Edward Fox and Rex Harrison. Fifty-odd years previously, Muth had entered a radio competition and won first prize: two tickets to the then brand new Broadway musical, *My Fair Lady*, starring a much younger Rex Harrison. Heavily pregnant at the time, Muth treasured that great event in her early married life. Rex Harrison had remained her decided favorite ever since.

As Joanie and I waited for the actors to emerge, I was clutching a birthday card for Muth, which we were hoping Mr. Harrison would agree to sign.

Finally the stage door opened and a batch of extras came out. Next came Edward Fox, who looked slightly disappointed when all we did was nod and smile. But we had bigger fish to fry.

Suddenly, there he was. Eighty years old, and accompanied by a minder, Rex Harrison still retained that noble elegance that was so much a part of his presence over more than half a century on stage and screen. Joanie and I thanked him for that evening's performance, then made our request, describing our mother's longstanding admiration and the play that had initiated it. He took the card and pen; his attendant provided a clipboard for him to lean on, and Rex Harrison wrote a birthday greeting that Muth treasured until the day she died:

Happy birthday to a fair lady. Rex Harrison

That same year, Joanie and I had another memorable encounter, brazenly orchestrated by my letter to the then up and coming English actor, Alex Jennings, who was later to achieve considerable success in theater, movies, and television. We had tickets to see him in a matinee of *Too Clever by Half* in London's West End, which we were attending with an old family friend and theatre-lover, Audrey. My letter was an invitation for Mr. Jennings to join us for tea after the performance, and stressed how much it would mean to Audrey, our elderly companion, to meet him. I was amazed and delighted to receive a letter back from him, accepting the invitation!

We met Alex at the stage door and walked together to a nearby restaurant. Audrey had been appalled at what she felt was my audacity to invite an actor, a stranger, for tea with us. But she was quickly won over by his charm and complete lack of arrogance. For his part, Alex never appeared to question why he was visiting with three complete strangers without so much as a film contract among them. The four of us spent a pleasant hour together before we said our goodbyes.

When recovering from a stem cell transplant, and contending with C-Diff—on top of various other challenges to my health and well-being, meeting a public figure was at the bottom of my to-do list. Such memories, however, conjured up delightful encounters from before my world began to shrink. For that alone, I treasured them.

I knew my world was going to grow larger again—it had already begun to with every step I took into the great outdoors, every car journey, and every Zoom gathering or video call.

Memories of past joys are a powerful promise of joys still to come.

Thank you, Your Royal Highness and Sir Rex Harrison (RIP). Thank you, Sir Patrick Stewart. Thank you, Alex Jennings.

Thank you, God.

Chapter Forty-four: T-Day Plus Twenty-eight
Good Guys and Bad Guys

This morning, I was feeling utterly confused.

I had started taking my C-Diff antibiotic and the counteractive pro-biotic the previous afternoon, and I was already losing track of when to take what. For one thing, the antibiotic had to be taken every six hours, which meant that at least one dose was scheduled for the middle of the night, or the very early morning. That wasn't so bad—I usually woke up at an ungodly hour to pee—but it was complicated by the scheduling of the pro-biotic. That had to be taken either no less than an hour before the antibiotic, or no less than two hours after it. Otherwise, the antibiotic would simply kill it. On top of this, I still had my ten other medications and supplements to fit into each 24-hour period, and one of those was a prophylactic antibiotic which also might eat up the pro-biotic. It was nearly impossible to keep track of it all.

I wondered whether I should purchase one of those plastic pill holders marked with the hours of the day—but that would mean keeping an eye on both it and the clock every waking hour. Plus some of my sleeping hours. Maybe I could just eat yogurt... But my antibiotic would probably neutralize yogurt too. Instead, I drew up a little pill-taking schedule and set several alarms on my phone. Modern technology saved the day once again!

Modern technology was in its embryonic stage when I began my working life back in 1979. I was employed as a management trainee at a large, direct mail company, ending up in the marketing division after

18 months of placements in every department. Not surprisingly, the company's business relied on an enormous database of customers and prospects, and the computer array filled a ballroom-sized area with disc and tape drives. It's amazing to think that all that data would probably fit on a single laptop today. Possibly even a cellphone.

In those days, a team of programmers and operators was required, around the clock, to ensure that everything ran smoothly and that all those tantalizing mailings reached the homes of potential customers. "You may already have won a new car!" was one of the all-important messages—but first, why not purchase this book? Or set of records? Or magazine subscription? (You don't have to purchase the product in order to win, but we're counting on you to believe it will give you a better chance if you do...)

When I first moved to London, I was renting a room from an elderly couple, and I was desperate to have a place of my own. Unfortunately, I wasn't earning much, which limited my options considerably, but eventually I found an apartment over a pet store in a rather dubious part of north London.

My apartment was on the third and fourth floors of the building. The first floor was the pet store, and the second floor held two rooms full of noisy birds. But these were no ordinary birds. I was picking up dinner in a nearby fish and chip shop one evening, and the proprietor informed me that my landlord, Mike, the pet shop owner, was involved in an illegal operation, smuggling exotic birds into the country, thereby avoiding customs and quarantine regulations and fees. I decided not to mention my discovery to Mike, but I became extra vigilant, taking note of various dodgy-looking, cage-toting characters I occasionally ran into on my way up the stairs. One such character delivered a hawk one day, and, for the next week, I had to step over trays of dead chicks—dinner for the hawk—to reach the door to my apartment.

Not surprisingly, considering the amount of bird seed that littered the place, I had mice too. Lots of mice. I needed a cat. And one day I found one. Someone had abandoned a tiny, tortoiseshell kitten in the alleyway behind the building, probably assuming it would be taken in to be sold in the store. But the kitten wasn't exotic enough for that, so I claimed her instead. She stormed my heart, little Crickle, and, although she didn't prove to be much of a mouser, her mere presence in the apartment seemed to keep the mice at bay. Occasionally she did manage to catch one, but mostly she preferred to bat ping pong balls around the living room.

When it came to the necessary facilities, there was a strange set-up in my residence. The bathroom had a sink and a bath, but no toilet. The toilet was on the second floor, beyond the door to my apartment, in between two rooms full of birds and the omnipresent mice. One day I noticed a fat twist of wires, attached to the ceiling light above the toilet, and extending down the wall, through the floor, to the store below. "Strange," I thought, and then it hit me. The light in the toilet ran off our electricity supply, and our landlord, Mike, was tapping into it for his own use. I decided to test my theory that night, after the store was closed.

I flipped the switch on my apartment's electricity supply, then went down into the street and looked through the store windows. The whole building had gone dark. Our crooked landlord didn't just smuggle birds; he stole electricity, too.

The next morning, I called the police, and a young constable showed up a short time later. He sat down, put his cap on the floor next to him, and opened his notebook. He didn't actually say, "'ello, 'ello, 'ello,'" but he did ask, "Now, what's all this then?" As I was explaining the situation, Crickle sniffed at the policemen's cap, then went to sleep on it.

When I had finished telling my story, I asked the officer not to say anything to my landlord just yet because I was afraid of how he might react. I don't know what I thought I could do to keep myself safe, but I needed time to put some kind of protection in place. The policeman assured me that he wouldn't say a word, then he tipped Crickle off his cap, brushed away a few cat hairs, and departed.

He went straight down to the pet shop and told my landlord that I'd reported him for stealing our electricity.

Mike phoned a few minutes later and threatened to have my legs broken.

Thankfully, my legs remained in one piece, but my next move was to make an appointment with a lawyer at the local Citizen's Advice Bureau. I was sitting in his office, recounting my tale of woe, when one of his colleagues burst in. "Get out of the building!" he shouted, "It's on fire!"

We joined the rest of the occupants making a quick exit, then stood around outside, waiting for the firetruck, while, behind us, the establishment, a pre-fab building, went up in flames. After what seemed like hours, but was probably only around five minutes, the firefighters arrived, jumped off their truck, and ran in completely the wrong direction. My lawyer had to run after them and direct them to the blaze. Meanwhile, on the assumption that my appointment had been cancelled, I walked back to the apartment.

It wasn't only the cacophony of bird sounds, the mice, and the shady landlord that disturbed my peace; my building was two doors away from a dance hall that attracted crowds every Saturday night. And on most of those Saturday nights, at closing time, the hall would empty out into the street, where much shouting and fighting would erupt. The police would arrive, there would be a few arrests, and things would quiet down by around 2:00 AM.

One night, I heard what sounded like a car backfiring. The next thing I knew, the area outside the dance hall had been cordoned off and the street was full of police cars and emergency vehicles. I read in the paper the next day that a customer, who'd been banned from the premises, had returned with a sawn-off shotgun and killed the doorman.

Clearly it was time to look for another place to live, and I—having had enough of the ordeals of renting— decided to become a homeowner. My father was in the country on business at that time, and he devoted a couple of days to driving me around and viewing properties with me. One place in particular looked like a good candidate—a house that was being converted into two apartments. Dad particularly liked that one, but I decided the kitchen was too small. We crossed it off the list.

A few weeks later I saw that very house on the front page of the newspaper. It turned out that a serial killer had lived there before it was converted, and bits of bodies were buried in the basement and the back yard. Talk about dodging a bullet! I felt sorry for the people who had bought the apartments—but I was very glad I'd wanted a bigger kitchen.

Eventually I found my little railroad cottage in Surrey, and joined the ranks of commuters. By that time, Crickle had had a litter of five kittens, one of which I kept, so there I was, the crazy spinster cat lady that no neighborhood should be without.

A murder took place two doors from my apartment. My landlord threatened me with bodily injury. I survived a fire in a Citizen's Advice Bureau. And I nearly bought a house once occupied by a serial killer. All this happened within just a few months. None of these events, however, brought fear even close to what I felt when I was first diagnosed with a cancer that had a history of taking lives.

Then I met my doctors, who assured me that I would live to a ripe, old age.

I have no doubt that those doctors were channels for the greatest healer of all.

The words Jesus says to us, more than any others, are "Do not be afraid." With only two days to go before I reached the all-important T-Day plus thirty—when I would have survived the most challenging period of my recovery—I was full of gratitude for God's grace-filled provision, for my medical team, and for the continued care that convinced me I had no need to be afraid.

No doubt there would be plenty of reasons to be fearful in years to come, but mantle cell lymphoma was no longer one of them.

Chapter Forty-five: T-Day Plus Twenty-nine
Loud and Clear

In the list of instructions I was given on my discharge from the hospital, one of the items was to make a follow-up appointment with my primary care physician. For the past thirteen years, I'd been in the care of a wonderful doctor who, much to my regret, had recently accepted a new position and moved away. Her replacement was much older and male. I admit that I felt some trepidation about the change.

I needn't have worried. Kind, thoughtful, and very thorough, Dr Lavi took time to get to know me as a person, not just a patient. He was especially attentive to my C-Diff condition, and urged me to drink plenty of fluids—particularly electrolytes—in order to avoid dehydration.

Before the examination was over, Dr Lavi dictated his notes into the computer, including his description of me as "a lively and intelligent woman." I had to wonder what he dictates when the patient is a jerk.

Over my past sixty years, with its numerous moves, I have been blessed with wonderful doctors in every place I've lived. Because of my extensive medical history, those relationships have been essential. It's surprising that very few of the physicians I've chosen have been the result of recommendations. I could say they just happened, but I don't believe that is so.

Just as I experienced being drawn to my future office window, desk, and employer, many other events in my life have given me a powerful sense of God at work.

In the Church, the first position after seminary is often a curacy, serving under the supervision of an established priest—an arrangement that could be compared to an internship in the medical field. My curacy was due to finish in spring of 2000, and, since Michael and I were attempting to start a family, I hoped to move on to a part-time position.

One day I had to attend a meeting in a part of Surrey I had never visited. As I drove through a charming little village, complete with a cricket field on the central green, I spotted a beautiful stone church with a rectory next door. "I would love to work and live there," I thought to myself.

Two months later, the bishop called and asked me to consider a part-time position in a village parish. Sure enough, it was the church I'd driven past. A visit and interviews were arranged, and Michael and I soon moved into the rectory. I worked three days a week, and Alex joined the family a year later. Our joy was complete.

One day, out of the blue, Michael suggested that we consider moving to the USA. I still had two years left on my contract with the parish, but we had a month-long vacation coming up, when we'd be traveling around the western and northeastern states, visiting family and friends. We decided to keep our eyes open, during that time, for possible locations to live and work in those areas of the country, and to follow up, in a couple of years, on what was available— preferably near loved ones.

For a week in the middle of the trip, we stayed at a resort in Colorado with my parents and sister. That Sunday morning we attended a worship service at a local church. The moment we walked through the door, I knew it was the parish I was meant to serve. "This is it!" I whispered to Michael, and discovered that he was feeling the same certainty.

We had already decided to return to the same resort a year later for a family reunion and celebration of my parents' 50th wedding anniversary. When the service was over, I introduced myself to the priest, told him about the upcoming anniversary, and asked if I could preside at a renewal of marriage vows for my parents in his parish on that occasion. He readily agreed.

As my family and I departed, I bubbled over with the joy of having found the parish I felt sure I was destined for. Although I hadn't said anything of the sort to the priest, Michael, my parents and my sister shared in my excitement. We planned that I would put out feelers when my existing contract finished in two years. In the meantime, we had another visit on the calendar for my parents' big day, the following year.

Two weeks later, when Michael and I were back home in England, I received a fax from my mother. She sent an advertisement she had cut out of Living Church for a part-time Associate Priest at the very parish in Colorado! I emailed the rector that day, reminding him of the conversation we'd had about my parents' renewal of vows, and expressing my interest in the Associate position. He responded immediately, asking for my resume.

On Thanksgiving Day, the Senior Warden interviewed me over the phone. We chatted and laughed for nearly an hour. It probably helped that I'd had a glass of wine with my turkey! We then entered the busy season of Advent, Christmas, and Annual Meetings, but in early February, I was invited to Colorado for in-person interviews with the rector and the vestry, which is the lay leadership of the parish.

I hopped onto a plane again and traveled to the snowy Rockies. That Sunday I was the guest preacher—so they could check me out—and I had two days of tours and interviews with the rector and other key personnel. The Senior Warden and his wife hosted me in their home, where we continued the lighthearted conversation we had initiated by phone on Thanksgiving Day.

The rector offered me the position as he drove me to the airport for my return flight, and Michael, Alex, and I moved to Colorado six months later, as soon as Alex's adoption was final. When we celebrated Muth and Dad's 50th anniversary, their renewal of vows took place in my church, and their party was in my parish hall.

However, as I familiarized myself with the parish finances, it became clear to me that the budget could not stretch to a second clergyperson—not even part-time. Because of this development, I began training for a license in interim ministry, and, after two years, I accepted a contract with a neighboring parish. When I'd completed that appointment, I was called to another interim position, in California, again for two years.

By this time, Alex was in first and second grade, and we didn't want her to have to keep changing schools every couple of years. The time had come for me to find a permanent rectorship.

The Episcopal Church has a system of matching clergy profiles with parish profiles—along the same lines as computer dating. When I started my search for a parish, I discovered that my profile was a perfect match with St. Catherine's, on the other side of the country. Like me, St. Cat's believed in fostering and equipping lay ministry, in active outreach to the community, in providing effective spiritual enrichment, in offering compassionate pastoral care, and serving the needs of all ages.

One of the elements of the parish profile was a video describing the parish's history and activities. At the end of the video, a parishioner—an elderly woman who was clearly a pillar of the community—gave a description of their ideal qualities in a rector. She listed a strong and visible faith, a pastoral heart, a sense of humor, a concern for the needs of low income and homeless individuals, a love of liturgy and music. Every quality she mentioned resonated with me, and when she finished by asking, "Do you think this might be you?" I answered my computer screen out loud.

"Yes!" I said, "I think it might be!"

I went through the usual round of telephone interviews (no video calls in those days), then Michael, Alex, and I were invited to visit the parish in the middle of a cold and snowy February. The weather was no deterrent, however. The moment I walked through the door for my first interview, I experienced that, by now, familiar sense that I was exactly where God wanted me to be. I was home.

That feeling of belonging was so powerful that I was tempted to tell the search committee that their search was over, but I managed to keep my mouth shut. In early May, two members of the committee came to California to see me in action in my parish, and I received the call to St. Cat's two weeks later.

If there is one thing I've learned in life, it's that God doesn't mess around. If we pay attention, we will know where we are meant to be, what we are meant to be doing, and how to be the best we can be.

In the months since I'd begun my enforced medical leave, not a day had gone by without my experiencing pangs of loss. I had spent nearly fourteen years doing what I was called to do, in a place I was called to be, and, throughout that time, I had tried hard to do my very best for my beloved parish. My precipitous departure felt like an abandonment—and yet, every day, through cards and emails, through the weekly newsletter, through updates conveyed during visits from parishioners and clergy colleagues, I was reassured that my ministry had borne fruit. My legacy to St. Cat's was an affirmation that her members were where they were meant to be, doing their very best to achieve what God had created them to do.

It was time to let go and concentrate on getting better.

Chapter Forty-six: T-Day Plus Thirty
Rules are Made to be Broken

It had arrived! The day had finally arrived: I was thirty days post-transplant, and I was alive and kicking. My temperature was normal, my blood counts were inching up to acceptable levels, and I could climb the stairs without pausing halfway to catch my breath. Best of all, I was not in the hospital— and I fully intended to keep it that way.

The reason the thirty-day milestone is so crucial is that, during that first four-week period, the levels of protective cells in the blood of a transplant patient are still too low to fight off any infection that might enter the body. My recent admission to the hospital, and intravenous antibiotics, were a response to that danger—and I would still have to be very careful about contact with other people, or with places where germs might linger—but I was out of the darkest part of the woods, and it was a great feeling.

To celebrate, I broke the rules and did something reckless—feeling not a stitch of remorse.

Robyn, and two other college friends, Sue and Paula, were having a mini-reunion in Connecticut, where Paula's mother lives—and Robyn and her family do too. Sue had flown in from Illinois to spend a couple of weeks with Paula, and the two of them had traveled down from Maine. With everyone in such close proximity, we'd agreed to take full advantage and to meet up for lunch at a central point.

Restaurants were still on my list of no-nos, because of the crowds, and the danger of eating food prepared and served somewhere other than my own kitchen.

But Robyn made special arrangements so that I could avoid those risks. She found a restaurant with outdoor seating and reserved a table at the very edge of the space overlooking the Connecticut River. She also explained my situation to the restaurant manager and received permission for me to bring my own food. With these special accommodations, I felt comfortable with my delinquency. Michael and I set off that morning full of happy anticipation.

We were the last to arrive, which meant that I could see all three of my beloved friends long before we got to the table. It felt like going back in time: the three of them looking, for all the world, no different from our shared college days. Oh, maybe a gray hair or two in the bunch—for those of us who had hair, that is—but the faces, those dear, familiar faces were just the same. The group radiated happiness. Since they hadn't spotted us yet, I could watch as Sue related a story and Paula and Robyn burst out laughing, then competed to get a word in for stories of their own.

Michael and I made our way to the table and joined in the frivolity.

I had put on a hat to protect my still sparse scalp from the sun. It was a flat, wide-brimmed, straw hat, which had fit me perfectly when I had hair. Unfortunately, the hat was now too big and rested on my ears. My ears, in return, were obligingly bending outwards to support the oversized headdress. I looked like a goat.

Thankfully our table, as well as being outdoors and at the edge of the seating area, was under a canvas roof: I could remove my hat without fear of sunburn. What I could not do, because of the germ risk, was hug my friends. That was difficult for me because this was the first time in several months that I'd seen Robyn, and years since I'd seen Sue and Paula.

But in a strange and lovely way, the mere presence of my friends felt like a hug—an all-encompassing, warm, and loving hug. These dear women had been by my side—albeit remotely—throughout my treatment and recovery. They had shared their lives with me, so I could think about things other than the four confining walls of a hospital room. They had comforted me when I was in pain, or undergoing gastric distress, or simply feeling blue; they had been a daily source of support, encouragement, and, above all, laughter. Now they were doing it all in person. My cup of joy was overflowing.

The one male in the group was, of course, my everlovin' husband. I couldn't have made the two-hour trip on my own, but Michael is a willing driver. He is so much more than that. From the moment I was first diagnosed, he has been at my side—sometimes from a distance, usually physically, always attentively. When, due to frustration or fear, I lashed out at him, he sometimes lashed back. We're only human, after all. Mostly he did his best to help me feel better. He'd made me copious cups of tea, coffee, and soup over the past nine months. He'd fetched, carried, and driven. He'd pushed me along lumpy sidewalks in a wheelchair that had seen better days. He'd told me I was beautiful on numerous occasions when the mirror said ... otherwise.

Now, sitting across from me on that gorgeous late spring day, surrounded by some of my dearest friends—who'd become his friends, too—Michael opened my thermos of soup for me, and everyone started eating. He gave me one of his French fries, because Michael always shares his food with me.

We had a lot of catching up to do with Robyn, Sue, and Paula. Children had grown up, some had married, some had moved out, some had stayed home. Husbands were complained about, and praised—and, in Sue's case, mourned.

Paula and Michael were still employed, but the rest of us were retired. For Robyn and Sue, that meant working hard on their respective yard and house projects. For me, it meant not doing very much—other than writing a book.

We took photographs of our happy reunion, and shared family photos from our phones. Those families included pets. Paula's husband and daughter had each adopted a Cavalier King Charles Spaniel from the same litter—two adorable little bundles who reminded me of Ernie in his early puppy days. We had left Ernie at home, of course. There's a limit to how accommodating a restaurant can be.

The five of us had so much to talk about that we outstayed our welcome at the table, and the restaurant host had to ask us to vacate it for the next party. But we found a little seating area by the parking lot and continued our conversation there—with me, under my hat, looking like a goat again.

All too soon, it was time to depart. We found it difficult to leave each other's company, but Paula had to get back to her mother. Meanwhile, my energy was beginning to flag. It may have been a triumphant thirtieth day post-transplant, but it was still only thirty days!

It's fitting that, as I reached the end of one of the most demanding periods of my life, I did so in the company of four people who had accompanied and supported me throughout those forty-one days—as well as the months leading up to them. They'd been with me from the moment of my diagnosis, with five decades of friendship, and nearly thirty years of marriage sustaining us.

I couldn't have done it without them.

274

Epilogue
Lessons Learned

I spent six weeks pre- and post-transplant focused on getting the most out of my treatments, but I had also spent that time reminiscing on a full, often fascinating, frequently amusing, past.

Shortly after the day of my transplant, I started writing about my experience, the people involved, and my state of mind and health. Those forty-one days, pre- and post-transplant, comprised such a significant period in my life, that I felt compelled to put it into words. As I wrote, I realized that my observations were leading me into memories, philosophizing, and spiritual reflection.

My words began to form themselves into a stream of consciousness that touched on much more than my immediate surroundings and condition. By the time I arrived back home again, it was clear that a book was materializing, and I committed to writing a chapter a day.

Paths emerge when one looks back over one's life. Thanks to my musings It had become clear to me how many of my paths had converged, diverged, intersected, changed direction, and progressed, to bring me to where I was on that sunny spring day with my husband and friends.

Although my rectorship had come to an abrupt end, I had discovered that my ministry was still going strong. It was just different. My changed circumstances, with their accompanying losses and other challenges, meant that I had to rely on the ministry of other people much of the time. Yet I still had the capacity to respond to the needs of those same people.

Never had it been so apparent to me that ministry is reciprocal.

At BWH, Florence administered my medications, dealt with my commode, and did her best to answer my many questions. In return, I listened to her stories, her complaints, and her advice.

Several other nurses and nursing assistants and students tended to me as well. They took my vital signs, changed my sheets, and brought me drinks. In return I encouraged and complimented them. Most important, I also thanked them.

The various members of service staff who came into my hospital rooms to empty trash, mop the floors, remove food trays, and take care of whatever else needed doing, invariably brightened my day with their cheerful greetings and their earnest dedication to their work. I hope I made it clear to them how very much I valued and appreciated their presence.

Ministry does not require one to wear a piece of plastic around one's neck. I certainly never sported one with my johnny—or even when I got dressed in real clothes. Ministry doesn't even require a person to profess a faith—although I'm sure there are many who would disagree. I have seen too many acts of kindness and generosity, motivated by nothing more than the desire to ease another person's journey through life's challenges, to believe otherwise.

My memories of unpleasant experiences, errors of judgment, failed relationships, and heartbreaking losses, are vastly outweighed by the other kind. What strikes me most when I look back over nearly 70 years of precious, unpredictable life, is a tangible awareness of God's presence and guidance. Many of my encounters, over those years, were with kind, genuine people—some of whom are household names. I'm grateful that I learned valuable lessons, and visited remarkable places.

Through it all, I was blessed by the shared affection and laughter of my ever-widening circle of loved ones.

This priest was taken out of her church—but church will never be taken out of this priest. I don't need to be wearing vestments and standing at an altar to be a member of God's church; I only need to pay attention. I only need to use this body God has made whole, and this heart that has never stopped loving, to make a difference—whatever my circumstances, and wherever I am called to be.

And that, dear reader, is the bald truth.

Acknowledgements

If not for the encouragement of those friends who brightened up my days with their messages of support, Bald might never have come to be. My texts to them were full of the kind of observations that eventually made their way into these pages. In return, my friends would often say those magic words: "You should write a book!" So I did.

As the chapters accumulated, a cherished team of proofreaders played their part in hunting out typos and suggesting changes. My sister, Joanie, my husband, Michael, and my dear friend Robyn, diligently read through the manuscript—more than once—and helped to make it as clean as it could be.

Joanie gave me the greatest gift of all when she introduced me to my wonderful editor, Sally Fagan Greenberg. Sally is extremely good at what she does, and is a delight to work with. *Bald* is a better book due to her thoughtful suggestions. More than that, over the course of several months we spent working together, Sally has become a treasured friend.

But it doesn't stop there. Sally introduced me to her friend Joel Seligmann, a talented artist, who produced the evocative artwork for the cover of Bald. My life is richer for having Sally and Joel in it.

My beloved husband, Michael, is so much more than a skilled proofreader. He has been by my side throughout one of the greatest ordeals of my life. Even when he was at the other end of a phone, he lightened my load, loved me unconditionally, and made me laugh.

I don't have far to look to see the blessings in my life.

www.ingramcontent.com/pod-product-compliance
Lightning Source LLC
La Vergne TN
LVHW051824080426
835512LV00018B/2713